Money and the Gospel

Financial Planning
for the Glory of God

WALDEAN WALL

moneyandthegospel.com

◉

MONEY AND THE GOSPEL

Copyright © 2018 by Waldean Wall

ISBN: 987-0-692-12751-3

No one can serve two masters, for either he will hate the one and love the other, or he will be devoted to the one and despise the other. You cannot serve God and money.

—MATTHEW 6:24—

DEDICATION

I thank God for my wife, Sheila,
and her continual love and support.
She is exactly what I need.

ACKNOWLEDGMENT

I would like to acknowledge my father,
who didn't have much money
but was rich toward God.

Contents

Introduction

Do Christians really need to think about their financial planning in a unique way? I'm guessing most would answer, "Absolutely." But if I went on to ask why and how we should think and plan differently, we may not have a good answer.

Some might say the main difference for a Christian is found in our giving. We should give to our churches and fund Christian efforts. While giving is important, the biblical approach to giving may be much different than you think.

Others might say the difference is in how we invest. We shouldn't invest in companies that promote alcohol, gambling, pornography, and so on. While there's a big difference in where and how Christians should invest, that's not the biggest factor in a Christian approach to financial planning.

It's common to think that the big thing for Christians is to stay out of debt. The borrower is a slave to the lender (Proverbs 22:7), right? While this too is good, many secular financial planners will also give this advice.

What's really important is much simpler than giving more, investing appropriately, and staying out of debt. For the Christian, financial planning isn't so much about following a list of rules; it's about being consumed by the gospel and living out what we believe. After all, God's mercy and grace in Jesus is at the core of who we are and what we live for.

Here's an overview of the five steps in creating a gospel-centered vision and plan for your money:

Step 1: **Connect the gospel to our money.** Since the gospel changes everything, it's important to understand how it impacts our finances and our planning. Thinking about money rightly and handling money the way we should is more than simply being disciplined or conservative.

Step 2: **Absorb the biblical perspective.** Since believing the gospel gives us new hearts for God, understanding his perspective is critical as we formulate our planning and make financial decisions. Biblical instruction, warnings, and examples give us what we need to think about and handle money as we should.

Step 3: **Be aware of the struggles.** Since following Jesus is a life of joy and challenge, there will be obstacles that get in the way. Understanding the struggles that will come can help us spot them and respond rightly. Among the seven topics we address here are faith and finances, your unique financial path, fear, and planning for retirement.

Step 4: **Face real questions.** Even if our motives are good, the call to follow Jesus will raise difficult questions that must be answered if we're to keep moving forward. We can be stumped even when our hearts are right. Among the nine questions we'll tackle here are questions about tithing, saving for retirement, owning stock, debt, how to think about purchases, and the challenge of differing financial priorities for those who are married.

Step 5: **Take action.** Here we'll look at ten strategies that can help you create a financial plan for the glory of God. Since any desire to improve or change is a call to action, this is critically important.

It's my hope that this resource will be a means through which God will develop us into a people who have a joyful, radical vision for following Jesus with everything we are and everything we have.

1

Connecting Money and the Gospel

Creating a Solid Foundation

As the first step to winning the money battle, understanding and being captured by the gospel is critical. Many Christians function from a list of dos and don'ts that, over time, tend to create a separation between what they do and why they do it. If we focus on the things we're doing or not doing, it becomes easy to find more value in our actions than in the One who saved us.

While obedience is vital, in our conversion the Holy Spirit actually changes the heart so we can believe in, align with, and love Jesus. Because of the gospel, we can and should construct our financial plan on our life in Christ. In our being united with Christ, God's vision becomes our vision, and the beauty of the gospel pulls new priorities from us.

When it comes to finances, there's much more at stake than creating a budget or paying off debt or giving money to the church. We've been rescued so that we'll live in a way that follows the One, "who gave himself for us to redeem us from all lawlessness and to purify for himself a people for his own possession who are zealous for good works" (Titus 2:14).

The apostle Peter put it like this: "Let your manner of life be worthy of the gospel of Christ" (Philippians 1:27).

The way we live should reflect the gospel's true worth. And the reality is that our lives—including our finances—reflect the value we place on the gospel. If the gospel is worth relatively little to us, our lives will show that. And if the gospel is our consuming treasure, our lives will show that as well.

THE GOSPEL CHANGES EVERYTHING

The best expression of who God is was demonstrated two thousand years ago when Jesus, the perfect One, absorbed the consequence of our sin on the cross. In the death of Jesus, we see God's justice – he dealt with sin. We also see God's love – Jesus gave himself for us. Jesus's death means I'm now God's friend and not his enemy. Receiving the gospel creates indescribable joy in those who believe while also bringing God the glory he deserves.

God is our caring Father who always works for our good. Jesus is our all-sufficient, saving brother who intercedes for us. And the Spirit of Christ is moving us toward becoming like Jesus. In spite of our being dead toward God – no pulse – Jesus's death gives us new life so we can embrace the treasure that is God himself:[1]

For our sake [God] made [Jesus] to be sin who knew no sin, so that in him we might become the righteousness of God. (2 Corinthians 5:21)[2]

The gospel changes everything. Through faith in Jesus and his cross-work, we move...

from death to life (Colossians 2:13).

from being far away to being near (Ephesians 2:13).

from being divided to being united (Ephesians 2:15).

from hostility to peace (Ephesians 2:16-17).

from being aliens to being citizens (Ephesians 2:19).

from being slaves of sin to being slaves of righteousness (Romans 6:17-18).

When God opens the heart to the true nature of sin and the beauty of Jesus, we believe and gain eternity with Christ – starting here and now. And with a new heart that is free from the demands of sin, we can become who we were created to be – people who are zealous for the good works that show Jesus's value.

This massive transformation within us changes everything about us as the Spirit reworks our lives to align them with the reality of our new birth. We're now called to joyfully follow the biblical examples of those who, in faith, turned away from sin to follow God. We show the worth of Jesus by declaring the gospel, feeding the hungry, clothing the naked, contributing to the needs of the saints, using our spiritual gifts, praying for those in need, raising our children for the sake of Jesus, and suffering with Christ rather than hoping in the pleasures of this world.

In 1 John 5:3-4 we see that the work of the gospel in us—being born of God—means that we overcome the world. For the Christian, following Jesus may not be easy, but it shouldn't be a burden. Our hearts should be longing to follow him:

> For this is the love of God, that we keep his commandments. And his commandments are not burdensome. For everyone who has been born of God overcomes the world. (1 John 5:3-4)

The term *overcome* in this passage means there will be many difficult battles as we prayerfully strive to live as we should.

Jesus tells us that those who would follow him cannot hold on to this life and its false promises. They must lose what once held life's purpose, and find fulfillment in him:

For whoever would save his life will lose it, but whoever loses his life for my sake will find it. (Matthew 16:25)

Here is the apostle Paul's understanding of his purpose as he pursued and finished his mission to spread the good news of Jesus:

I do not account my life of any value nor as precious to myself, if only I may finish my course and the ministry that I received from the Lord Jesus, to testify to the gospel of the grace of God. (Acts 20:24)

For the Christian, financial planning is not primarily about strategies and tactics. It's all about being a disciple of Jesus and walking by faith. For us, everything—including the way we handle money—is now a means to glorify God. Our burning desire must be for our money to serve the purpose of the One who gave himself for us.

BELIEF IS SEISMIC CHANGE

Thinking about money in a new way can be a daunting and scary proposition. It's never easy to move from finding our security in money to depending on God and his promises. Living as a steward rather than an owner is difficult.

But be encouraged; the biggest change you'll ever make has already been made. You believe the gospel. God has removed your hard-as-stone heart and given you one that believes in and trusts a life-changing reality that most people reject. You understand the crushing reality of your sin and have turned to Jesus. You've embraced him as the One who was judged in your place so you could be forgiven. This God-wrought faith is a seismic departure from the norm. It's a miracle. So take heart! Saving faith means you have a new life (2 Corinthians 5:17).

Saving Faith Produces Change

Our lives are built on what we believe, right? Pretty much everything we do emerges from what we embrace as true. Our priorities and actions are linked to the truths we trust.

Real faith is not simply passive, mental assent. Faith is commitment to a reality. Real faith can be seen by the change that comes from it.

This concept was important to James. He wanted his readers to know that faith goes hand in hand with change and action:

So also faith by itself, if it does not have works, is dead. (James 2:17)

Faith apart from works is useless. (2:20)

For as the body apart from the spirit is dead, so also faith apart from works is dead. (2:26)

Believing the gospel – all that Jesus is for us – changes the way we think about everything, including our finances.

The Main Objective

While we all need to battle sin every day, the larger goal was summarized by Paul: we're to imitate Jesus.

Be imitators of me, as I am of Christ. (1 Corinthians 11:1)

Therefore be imitators of God, as beloved children. (Ephesians 5:1)

Because Jesus was all about bringing glory to God, that's *our* destiny too (John 12:28; 17:1). Jesus's life of self-sacrificing purity not only qualified him to take our place on the cross; it also showed us what our lives should be like.

Because we're no longer who we once were, we need to get rid of the defeated idols that stand in our way and slow us down. Christians die for the gospel because they have a treasure that's worth more than this life. Pastors and missionaries here and around the world spread the gospel while living in poverty because their treasure is more valuable than comfort.

For the believer, the gospel is connected to everything – including our money.

Change and Money

Since we've been redeemed from all our futile ways (Titus 2:4; 1 Peter 1:18) and now are being aligned with a new Jesus-is-Lord-over-everything vision of life, our attitude toward money must change so that it matches who we are in Christ. No more worshiping God's gifts rather than God himself. The saving work of Jesus makes it possible to see all of life in the context of the gospel.

Money and all that it represents is a major battleground for both the wealthy and the not-so-wealthy. It entices us to act as if we belong to this world, and as if we don't believe in Christ. It's no wonder that much of the Bible's teaching about money is in the form of warnings and absolutes like "You cannot serve God and money" (Matthew 6:24), or "It is easier for a camel to go through the eye of a needle than for a rich person to enter the kingdom of God" (Mark 10:25), or "Anyone of you who does not renounce all that he has cannot be my disciple" (Luke 14:33).

***

Faith and works are bound up in the same bundle. He that obeys God trusts God, and he that trusts God obeys God. He that is without faith is without works, and he that is without works is without faith.

– C. H. Spurgeon –

GOSPEL CHANGE IS COSTLY

Jesus knew the meaning of sacrifice in a way that we can't fully understand. Being innocent, he willingly absorbed the indescribable judgment that should have been ours. He endured the cross because he found joy in our happiness and joy in the glory that God would gain (Hebrews 12:2).

Jesus knew the cross was in his future, and he moved toward it with determination. His sacrifice didn't catch him by surprise, and he was remarkably clear about how his disciples would also face difficulties. He wanted those who follow him to understand what was in front of them.

The Cost for Us

What does it cost to follow Jesus?

In one sense, nothing. It's all gain. As we follow Jesus, any difficulty we encounter will serve us, because God works all things for our good (Romans 8:28). In another sense, however, following Jesus will cost everything, because we see life's new purpose.

When we were dead in our sins, we were aligned with the priorities and enticements of this world. But now, because we have a changed heart that's aligned with God, we encounter costs in making the shift from the temporal pleasures that bring death to the everlasting pleasures that come with the pursuit of eternal life.

Jesus spoke of cost in different ways. In Luke 14:26-33 we read this:

26If anyone comes to me and does not hate his own father and mother and wife and children and brothers and sisters, yes, and even his own life, he cannot be my disciple. 27Whoever does not bear his own cross and come after me cannot be my disciple. 28For which of you, desiring to build a tower, does not first sit down and count the cost, whether he has enough to complete it? 29Otherwise, when he has laid a foundation and is not able to finish, all who see it begin to mock him, 30saying, "This man began to build and was not able to finish." 31Or what king, going out to encounter another king in war, will not sit down first and deliberate whether he is able with ten thousand to meet him who comes against him with twenty thousand? 32And if not, while the other is yet a great way off, he sends a delegation and asks for terms of peace. 33So therefore, any one of you who does not renounce all that he has cannot be my disciple.

To all those who would follow him, Jesus here is saying this:

1. He must be your first love. (v. 26)

2. You will publicly display and confess your hope. (v. 27) Just as carrying a Roman cross was seen as a public display of Rome's rule over one's life, disciples live in a way that show's Jesus's rule over their lives.

3. This new path will claim everything. (vv. 28-32)

4. Following him includes committing everything to his purposes. (v. 33)

Pretty daunting, right? For the Christian, however, this shouldn't sound like something to dread. It should be something we long for. Anyone who knows the salvation of Christ, and who's a new person in that salvation (2 Corinthians 5:17; Galatians 2:20; Ephesians 2:10), should long to pursue the One who gives eternal joy. This daunting but beautiful aspiration is ours because we've found a treasure that's worth more than anything else (Matthew 13:44).

While following Jesus isn't easy, two things are very important here. First, we should have a desire to worship with everything we are and have. Second, putting the enticements of this world behind us is a process – the process of sanctification. It's the process whereby the indwelling Holy Spirit moves us closer and closer to the image of Jesus, and further and further away from lesser gods.

Applying This to Our Finances

Changing the way we think about our financial planning can be a painful thing. It's easy to develop an addiction to the temporal and often worldly benefits of money. We go to money to find comfort, power, entertainment, influence, security, approval, and a host of other things. It can be tough finding our satisfaction and purpose in God. There will be a cost.

Because it can be difficult to break our addiction to money and the things money can buy, it's important to keep our eyes on Jesus and all that he is for us. Money must become something used to bring glory to the One who is our supreme satisfaction.

If God would grant us the vision, the word "sacrifice" would disappear from our lips and thoughts; we would hate the things that seem now so dear to us; our lives would suddenly be too short; we would despise time-robbing distractions and charge the enemy with all our energies in the name of Christ.

– Nate Saint –

BEWARE OF EXCUSES

Because following God takes faith, and living a life of faith can be scary, I've noticed that it's easy to find excuses to delay our obedience or to say no to God. The Bible is full of examples of this. Adam used Eve as his excuse for sinning (Genesis 3:12-13). Saul used pressing circumstances to justify disobedience (1 Samuel 13:11-12). Moses (Exodus 4:10) and Gideon (Judges 6:15) wanted to be excused because they felt inadequate – or so they said. And Jesus exposed the lame excuses used by some (visiting a field, examining some oxen, being newly married) for not coming to the kingdom of God (Luke 14:15-20).

Following Jesus means he has first place in my life, and his priorities are my priorities. It means I give my life to him, depend on his care, and do what he asks of me.

In Luke 9:59-62, we read of two men receiving the most glorious command anyone could receive: Jesus said to them, "Follow me." And yet one man responds, "I'll do that after I bury my father," and the other man responds, "I'll do that after I say farewell to those at home."

I find two very interesting things about this. First, these responses seem extremely reasonable. And second, Jesus rejects them.

This short interaction in Luke can be confusing. Isn't it reasonable for people to focus on such important issues as these before they follow Jesus? After all, following Jesus means their lives will move in a new direction. The point of this story, however, is that those who hear Jesus's call must and will follow. The call of Christ creates new hearts that follow him.

The men in Luke 9 said, "Yes, *but first...*" Or in other words, "I'll do it later." But Jesus was saying you can't put off his call to follow.

The call to be a disciple of Jesus is not simply mental assent. It's not, "That sounds great, and I'll deal with it after the important stuff of life." When Jesus calls, we believe, and we're changed. And belief empowered by the Holy Spirit will produce new priorities. True conversion means that the foundation of my life has changed, and now I deal with life as I follow Jesus.

The response of the two men showed that their lives had not changed from the inside. It showed that other things were more important than following Jesus.

For those who don't see with new eyes, Jesus said many things that can seem unreasonable:

> If anyone would come after me, let him deny himself and take up his cross and follow me. (Matthew 16:24)

> Any one of you who does not renounce all that he has cannot be my disciple. (Luke 14:33)

> Whoever loves his life loses it, and whoever hates his life in this world will keep it for eternal life. (John 12:25)

How we use the money God has entrusted to us is a reflection of how we've absorbed the gospel. Those who would follow Jesus should not have divided interests. God's plan is for our good and his glory. The question is, will we follow? Will we trust him? Will we focus on his unshakable promises, or will we go our own way?

SPIRITUAL VS. SECULAR

Even as Christians, living in this world can lead us to adopt an earthly vision for how things work. We can easily build two compartments for life – the spiritual and the secular. This leads to living as if some activities (being in church, reading the Bible, small group meetings, or praying with a friend) are spiritual and God-focused, while other activities (work, leisure, or thinking about money) are not.

We might find the occupation of pastor falling into the spiritual category, while that of truck driver would not. Your friends at church would fall into the spiritual relationships category while your friends at work would not. Praying with someone in pain would be a spiritual activity while disciplining the children is not.

When we're in the spiritual arena – where we assume God is present, interested, and working – we can easily adopt a thoughtful, loving, contemplative, and caring personality. In the secular arena we might think and act differently; we function as if God is uninterested or not there.

When we use a God's-not-interested compartment, we adopt a worldly perspective that focuses on self. Living with this type of division can remove God from most of life.

A False Reality

The truth is that this spiritual-secular division is a false reality. Life in Jesus doesn't have this separation. The gospel is meant to dominate every area of life:

> You shall love the Lord your God with all your heart and with all your soul and with all your strength and with all your mind, and your neighbor as yourself. (Luke 10:27)

The apostle Paul did not embrace the spiritual-secular division. He wanted to do everything for the glory of God. Even the regular and mundane things of life are to reflect God's value:

> Whether you eat or drink, or whatever you do, do all to the glory of God. (1 Corinthians 10:31)

The thing is, unifying life under the gospel is critical if we're going to live as we should and impact this world for Jesus. If we yield pieces of life to a separate secular compartment, those pieces will weigh us down in compromise. They'll continually fight against Jesus living in us as he should.

Money and the Spiritual-Secular Divide

One of the most common spiritual-secular divisions is found in the way we think about money and our financial planning. By putting money and money decisions in the secular category, we get away from thinking like a steward, and we'll inevitably make wrong decisions.

It's easy to fall into this way of thinking. For example, it's easy to think that the money I give to the church belongs to God and the rest belongs to me. This is unbiblical, because all we have belongs to Jesus.

The battle to think about money in a Christ-exalting way is difficult because money opens the door to so much of what this world has to offer. Money temptations can connect to almost every aspect of life and call to us to think about self rather than God or others.

I place no value on anything I have or may possess, except in relation to the kingdom of God. If anything will advance the interests of the kingdom, it shall be given away or kept, only as by giving or keeping it I shall most promote the glory of Him to whom I owe all my hopes in time or eternity.

– David Livingstone –

APPLICATION

Before moving on, answer the following application questions. Also, review and complete the "Financial Priorities Report" in the appendix at the end of this book. This should take only a couple of minutes.

1. Give an example of a major change salvation has created in your life.

2. Give an example of how you struggle with the way you think about money.

3. Give an example of the sacred-secular division in your life.

2

Absorb the Biblical Perspective

Believing God's Vision for You and Your Money

Knowing what the Bible has to say about money is the second step in creating a Christ-exalting financial plan. With the guidance of the Holy Spirit, believers are in a position to receive warnings, instruction, and examples with anticipation. These will bring us closer to the goal of showing the value of Christ in our planning:

> All Scripture is breathed out by God and profitable for teaching, for reproof, for correction, and for training in righteousness, that the man of God may be complete, equipped for every good work. (2 Timothy 3:16-17)

Money is a gateway through which we experience much of life. With enough money, I can eat steak instead of hamburger. More money means I can drive a new Cadillac instead of a ten-year-old Chevy. And even more money means I can have a wonderful large home in a nice neighborhood rather than a small apartment in a rough part of town.

Since so much of life connects to money, it's no wonder the Bible has much to say about it. But why would the Bible talk so much about money and wealth? Well, maybe there's a strong relationship between how we think about our finances and living as a disciple. The gospel aligns the lost with God's vision for all of life, including how to think about and handle money. And the Bible gives us an understanding of the what, why, and how to move forward.

I imagine you would have little problem accepting the words of Jesus from Matthew 5:27-28 if you heard them preached this coming Sunday at your church: "You have heard that it was said, 'You shall not commit adultery.' But I say to you that everyone who looks at a woman with lustful intent has already committed adultery with her in his heart." From this text, we could examine the deep need for a holy mind or see the insidious nature of sexual temptation. We could look at David and Bathsheba, or at our tendency to use people rather than to serve them, or a host of other applications. Wherever we go with this passage, it would be challenging, convicting, and valuable. And I'm guessing we would agree on the biblical position on these things.

If, however, I preached on Luke 14:33, "So therefore, any one of you who does not renounce all that he has cannot be my disciple," you might be inclined to pay attention in a surely-that-can't-be-taken-literally way. Or you might assume that the passage means we need to be willing to renounce all that we have if God moves us to do that, but we don't *actually* need to renounce our possessions. I would have to be careful as I walked through the text before I suggested anything too radical. And hopefully, we wouldn't get to Luke 12:33 or 18:22.

God doesn't mince words when it comes to how we should view money. It's important, and it's clear. We, however, need hearts that long to follow.

STEWARDSHIP VS. OWNERSHIP

As we think about our financial planning, it's easy to absorb cultural concepts and norms without spotting the biblical conflict. Doing this is dangerous, as it creates thought patterns that are difficult to break. One of these unbiblical concepts is ownership. As Christians, we should think differently about possessions or talent or health or anything we're tempted to own. We should spend more time thinking about being *stewards* rather than owners.

But why is ownership so important to us? Think deeply. Is it that we want to operate autonomously? Is it that we feel good when we own stuff or have control? Is it that we want to leave God out of some area of life? If not, why do we resist the concept of God's ownership and our stewardship?

This is difficult. Biblical stewardship means that all of life should always be lived out in a way that brings joy to the King. In God's economy, we're continually operating within the sphere of his sovereign rule. We and everything we have belongs to him, and our "ownership" is never autonomous.

We didn't receive God's grace so that we can own more or take the credit for God's work. Because all things are from God and for God (Romans 11:36), we won't be able to live for Jesus as we should without embracing stewardship – using God's gifts for God's glory. This is a foundational concept when it comes to thinking about money.

Everything Belongs to God

From the first verse in the Bible, we see the foundation for stewardship: "In the beginning, God created the heavens and the earth" (Genesis 1:1). This is all we should need. Because God created everything that exists, everything that exists is his. And he has never relinquished that ownership. From the beginning of the Bible until the end, we know that God reigns:

> For from him and through him and to him are all things. To him be glory forever. (Romans 11:36)[3]

Financial stewardship begins with a deep understanding that God owns everything and is sovereign over everything. But, we have a serious "mine" problem, don't we? This house is mine. This car is mine. This 401(k) is mine. These children are mine. We just think like that. We desire to own stuff.

Here's the key: we can't be stewards of God's resources if we want to own God's resources. That's covetousness (wanting what belongs to someone else) or idolatry (finding satisfying purpose in something other than God). But we know that if something belongs to someone else – in this case, God – we can't do with it whatever we want. Being captivated by what belongs to God is indeed a great sin. Every dollar we earn and every asset we count as ours really belongs to God:

> So therefore, any one of you who does not renounce all that he has cannot be my disciple. (Luke 14:33)

And, by the way, if you're a Christian, you also belong to God. The gospel is the good news that you were bought with a price (1 Corinthians 6:20) and were redeemed from Satan's hand (Matthew 20:28; Acts 20:28). This way of thinking repulses many. We're bent on thinking about life in an autonomous way. We own, and we're in control. But this couldn't be further from the truth.

All "good" Christians will acknowledge God's ownership. But mental assent is not belief. We can find out if we truly believe this by looking at how we live, because we live out what we believe. Real stewards will stop thinking that their money belongs to them. God's ownership of that money will be top-of-mind in their planning.

God Gives Us Everything We Have

One of the great presumptuous sins of humanity is the thinking that we create success and influence and wealth. This is completely false. The blessings we have, even if we worked to acquire them, are all from God's hand.

Have you ever wondered why you were born where you were born, or how you come to have the talents you have, or the intellect, or the opportunities, or the health, or the money? Everything comes from the hand of God, even if we work hard.

King Nebuchadnezzar's great sin was thinking that he was the origin of all he had:

> And the king answered and said, "Is not this great Babylon, which I have built by my mighty power as a royal residence and for the glory of my majesty?" (Daniel 4:30)

What arrogance! But we are susceptible to this as well. It's easy to think I've accomplished great things on my own, or that the money in my 401(k) is there because of me. But everything we have comes from God's hand, and we cannot take credit for any of it. Nebuchadnezzar learned this through God's discipline. He ultimately confessed God's control: "All those who walk in pride he is able to humble" (Daniel 4:37).

> A person cannot receive even one thing unless it is given him from heaven. (John 3:27)[4]

If God owns everything and graciously gives us what we need, we should live lives of faith that depend on his care. We should believe his promises and instruction and focus on the mission. This doesn't mean we shouldn't work diligently. We should. But we should all be working for God's glory and not for our own glory. We must be faithful in our God-given responsibilities – honest and faithful to our employer, caring for our family, financially supporting missions, etc. – but we aren't working so we can have more "mine":

> Therefore do not be anxious, saying, "What shall we eat?" or "What shall we drink?" or "What shall we wear?" For the Gentiles seek after all these things, and your heavenly Father knows that you need them all. But seek first the kingdom of God and his righteousness, and all these things will be added to you. (Matthew 6:31-33)

Our Ultimate Role as a Steward

Wouldn't it be helpful if God would just get very specific on this? What exactly should a steward do?

Well, God has very specific instruction. He wants us to function in a way that brings him glory. As a steward of all he's entrusted to us – our children, our time, our bodies, the gospel, and certainly our money – we're to handle it all so as to make Jesus look good:

> Whatever you do, work heartily, as for the Lord and not for men (Colossians 3:23)[5]

It's easy to make this overly complicated to the extent that we fail to face a simple truth: life in Christ is all about God's glory and not our own. That's what it means to be a faithful steward – bringing glory to God with God's resources.

So how should we handle money? We may not usually think about God's glory when we save for retirement or buy a house or go on vacation or think about college costs. But we should. Everything we do should serve him. *Everything.*

> So, whether you eat or drink, or whatever you do, do all to the glory of God. (1 Corinthians 10:31)

Having an ownership mentality creates problems if we're going to live for Jesus. Our interests are divided and our loyalties are split if we have a "mine" mind. Ownership thinking is wrong and tempts us with a self-centered disposition that defeats our call to serve Jesus with his resources.

If you hoard a thing for yourself, it will turn into spiritual dry rot, as the manna did when it was hoarded. God will never let you hold a spiritual thing for yourself; it has to be given back to Him that He may make it a blessing to others.

– Oswald Chambers –

WARNINGS

Biblical warnings are a blessing from God designed to care for us and urge us on. They move us in the right direction and make sure we don't become lazy about following Jesus. Through the power of the Holy Spirit, warnings bring us to repentance and give us the resolve to stay in the fight for holiness. Through warnings, the Holy Spirit creates a faithful disposition in us and moves us down the narrow path.

Even as Christians, it can be easy to brush these warnings aside. It's easy to assume that since we count ourselves "saved," we can relax and take our time when it comes to dealing with sin. We're all tempted to treat warnings like suggestions so we can enjoy this world's enticements while still hoping for God's favor in the end.

A casual response to biblical warnings means something is wrong. For example, Scripture is clear that those who persist in sexual immorality will not inherit the kingdom of God (1 Corinthians 6:9-10; Galatians 5:19-21; Ephesians 5:5). If we're comfortable preferring sexual sin to life in Christ, we should be concerned.

Warnings help point the lost to Christ, but God also uses warnings to keep his children. If we think the warnings don't apply to us, we're presuming on God's grace. And that can be deadly.

Warnings should put us on our knees in repentance so we can rise with new fuel for the fight for holiness. Warnings are a means by which God keeps his children faithful.

The Love of Money

The biblical authors warn us about the soul-crushing power of money. And some of the strongest warnings come from Jesus. Money can bring us power and comfort and influence and preferential treatment and entertainment and a host of other earthly benefits. It brings the strongest delusions this world can offer, and it can serve as a poisoned arrow in the quiver of evil.

Let's look at a few of those biblical warnings:

The love of money leads to temptation:

Those who desire to be rich fall into temptation, into a snare, into many senseless and harmful desires that plunge people into ruin and destruction. (1Timothy 6:9)

The love of money creates godless ambition:

He who loves money will not be satisfied with money, nor he who loves wealth with his income; this also is vanity. (Ecclesiastes 5:10)

The love of money means you're not loving God:

No one can serve two masters, for either he will hate the one and love the other, or he will be devoted to the one and despise the other. You cannot serve God and money. (Matthew 6:24)

The love of money leads to spiritual failure:

For the love of money is a root of all kinds of evils. It is through this craving [to be rich] that some have wandered away from the faith and pierced themselves with many pangs. (1Timothy 6:10)

The desire to be money-rich is at odds with seeing Jesus in a saving way and functioning as we should. If we think about money wrongly, we cannot embrace Jesus as our treasure, or trust him for our needs, or be faithful stewards.

Loving Money Means God Is Not Our God

In teaching us about faithfulness in the context of money, Jesus raised some unsettling questions:

If then you have not been faithful in the unrighteous wealth, who will entrust to you the true riches? And if you have not been faithful in that which is another's, who will give you that which is your own? No servant can serve two masters, for either he will hate the one and love the other, or he will be devoted to the one and despise the other. You cannot serve God and money. (Luke 16:11-13)

There are two main warnings here. First, if we're not faithful in handling earthly money as a steward, we won't receive true riches. Second, being devoted to money means that we'll despise God.

Reading these verses, I struggled with a question: What are the "true riches" Jesus speaks of here, and which I'll miss if I love money and don't handle it as a steward?

I found that many commentators don't really attempt to answer this question (maybe because they don't like the answer). Many others create a generalized answer that won't offend anyone. The real answer, the contextual answer, is difficult to receive. It's offensive unless your ambition is to focus on Jesus.

The key to the right answer is found in Jesus's concluding words in that passage. *We cannot serve God and money.* Being loyal to money

37

means we'll ultimately hate God. And hating God means our faith is not saving faith. So when we serve another master – money – everything Jesus could be for us becomes the "true riches" that we miss out on.

I think my real struggle with this answer is due to money's strong attraction. I'm always looking for a way to think about money that combines being a disciple with having earthly ambition.

When we cling to God's gifts instead of clinging to God, we're in trouble. If we're making sinful decisions with God's money, we're pushing away the Jesus-purchased design and blessings that walking by faith brings.[6]

Just to be clear, this doesn't mean that we buy our salvation by doing good things. Rather, salvation is a gift from God (Ephesians 2:8-9) that gives us our supreme joy and treasure and purpose and preference. When the gospel creates a new person, a Christ-exalting life emerges (Ephesians 2:10).

If you're spiritually stagnant, it could be that you're not faithful with your money. The way we handle money helps us know if we're aligned with God's heart. If we're serving money, we can't have the true riches that come with serving God (Ephesians 2:13).

Jesus's Money Instructions

Luke 16:11-13 follows Jesus's parable of a dishonest manager who was wasting his master's resources and was about to lose his position (16:1-8). In a panic, before he was put out on the street, this manager forgave others' debts owed to his master, so that these persons he helped would give him food and shelter when he was unemployed.

In an earthly setting, this servant was wrong to use his master's wealth to create the resources he would need when he had no money. But this is exactly what God wants us to do with his resources. We're good stewards if we use what we're entrusted with – in this case, money – to build treasures in heaven. And how do we do that? Jesus tells us:

> And I tell you, make friends for yourselves by means of unrighteous wealth, so that when it fails they may receive you into the eternal dwellings. (Luke 16:9)

In other words, we should be using God's resources to bring others into the kingdom so that when money has no value (after our lives here are over), we have all we will need there. Ultimately our joy is aligned with God's glory and purpose.

This concept isn't unique to Luke 16:9:

> Sell your possessions, and give to the needy. Provide yourselves with moneybags that do not grow old, with a treasure in the heavens that does not fail, where no thief approaches and no moth destroys. (Luke 12:33)

> They are to do good, to be rich in good works, to be generous and ready to share, thus storing up treasure for themselves as a good foundation for the future, so that they may take hold of that which is truly life. (1 Timothy 6:18-19)

Money Can Be a Barrier to Salvation

Following an encounter with a rich young man who sorrowfully turned away from the offer of eternal life, Jesus counseled his disciples:

> "Again I tell you, it is easier for a camel to go through the eye of a needle than for a rich person to enter the kingdom of God." When the disciples heard this, they were greatly astonished, saying, "Who then can be saved?" But Jesus looked at them and said, "With man this is impossible, but with God all things are possible." (Matthew 19:24-26)

In this statement Jesus is isolating the rich person as someone who has no hope apart from God's saving action. A camel certainly isn't making it through the eye of a needle.

This passage has bothered me. What is Jesus really doing here? Is a rich person more difficult for God to save? No, he's not saying that. He's saying that being rich includes a powerfully addictive seduction that must be broken.

Just before these verses, we read that a rich young man came to Jesus with a wonderful question: "What must I do to be saved?" It was asked sincerely by a "good" man who wanted to be right with God – as long as money could remain the man's first love. Jesus's answer was radical: "Sell what you possess and give to the poor, and you will have treasure in heaven; and come, follow me." The man walked away after hearing this answer. He came face-to-face with his deepest priority – and money won.

The message is clear. Following Jesus – being saved – includes a change in loyalties. You don't come to Jesus saying, "I want the salvation you offer as long as I don't need to change my beliefs or values or priorities or treasure." Jesus isn't just another thing in our busy lives. He's what life is about.

The rich man in the story firmly believed in his money. Though he appeared to be a wonderful example of the ideal person, his heart was closed to Jesus.

Interestingly, after Luke's account of this meeting (18:18-26), he includes the story of another rich man, Zacchaeus (Luke 19:1-10). It's a parallel story with a few major differences:

– Zacchaeus was a bad man – a tax collector – with a horrible public reputation.

– As a result of his encounter with Jesus, Zacchaeus released his wealth and had a desire to right the wrongs he'd committed.

– Jesus boldly affirmed the change in Zacchaeus: "He also is a son of Abraham" (19:9).

The way we relate to money exposes our heart. If your faith is in money, it's not in Christ. If your faith is in Christ, it's not in money.

Is the Idol of Money Different?

In some ways, money is different from other idols. While most addictions are seen as negative (pornography, alcohol, nicotine, etc.), money is different. This world revolves around money, its use, and its appeal. Everyone wants more money.

This creates a massive struggle for the Christian. And it's not just the worldly messaging we're bombarded with. Often churches are on board as well. A substantial movement in the "Christian" community has bought into a worldly view of money.

The only hope for a rich person is for God to change the heart. Without this, we'll love the gift and reject the Giver.[7] Only God can move us from trusting money to trusting Jesus.[8]

Let us all be on our guard against the love of money. The world is full of it in our days. The plague is abroad... We are all liable to the infection, from the least to the greatest. We may love money without having it, just as we may have money without loving it. It is an evil that works very deceitfully. It carries us captive before we are aware of our chains.

– J. C. Ryle –

INSTRUCTION

Thankfully, the Bible does more than warn us of tragedy and tell us what not to do. It also tells us what we should be doing. Biblical instruction works against the dangers we're warned about.

It's important to know that biblical instructions aren't simply suggestions we can follow if it feels good to do so. We have instruction so that the gospel can live in us and through us. Instructions are really loving commands designed to help us become like Christ.

Remember, the gospel saves us in every way. Because we're united with Christ when we first come to believe in him, our eternal life with Jesus is here and now as well as future. We were given radically new hearts that are designed to live for Jesus in everything. Jesus "gave himself for us to redeem us from all lawlessness and to purify for himself a people for his own possession who are zealous for good works" (Titus 2:14).

Focus on What Lasts

Why would anyone knowingly invest in a scam? Why would anyone give their life and money to an endeavor that will prove to be empty and destructive? Well, we're all tempted to embrace the shallow and temporary instead of what's foundational and eternal. Jesus teaches us to avoid that:

> Do not lay up for yourselves treasures on earth, where moth and rust destroy and where thieves break in and steal, but lay up for yourselves treasures in heaven, where neither moth nor rust destroys and where thieves do not break in and steal. For where your treasure is, there your heart will be also. (Matthew 6:19-21)

The two commands here are (1) don't lay up for yourselves treasures on earth, and (2) *do* lay up for yourselves treasures in heaven. These two commands bring out two questions: Should I accumulate anything here? And what does Jesus mean by "treasures in heaven"?

Don't Accumulate Treasure Here

This instruction demands that we prayerfully examine ourselves. What are we working for? What are we accumulating? What are we thinking about and hoping for? Is our treasure here? Is it obvious that we're focused on living as a disciple who embraces Jesus's mission?

We're not to focus on building treasure here. While this doesn't mean we shouldn't put money in a retirement plan, it does mean that the money in our retirement plan can't be our treasure. Now this is where it gets fuzzy. We don't want to be self-deceived and think that money isn't our treasure when it really is. We don't want to be like the unbelievers we read about in Titus 1:16 who professed to know God while denying him in their works.

Treasuring the wrong treasure is dangerous. It's idolatry. At a minimum, it shows that we don't grasp the grandeur of the gospel and we're spiritually immature. It may mean that since other things (like money) mean more to us than Jesus does, we don't actually know him in a saving way. Clinging to any treasure other than Jesus is clinging to a false god.

Anything we accumulate should cause us to be on guard. The security that money promises can easily move our eyes away from Jesus and tempt us to substitute being dependent on God with hope in the comfort that money can give.

Do Accumulate Eternal Treasure

This passage not only tells us to avoid pursuing temporary earthly treasure; it also instructs us to lay up eternal treasure. So how do you do that? Sell your possessions and give to the needy (Luke 12:33). Be full of good works, generous, and ready to share (1 Timothy 6:18). Use what God has entrusted you with to build the kingdom of God (Luke 16:9).

Remember, we're stewards of God's resources and not owners. We cannot have it both ways. We cannot treasure wealth here and be building eternal treasure at the same time. If we pursue reward here, the extent of our reward is whatever we get here (Matthew 6:2, 5, 16).

The fight to be faithful is not an easy one. It's a fight that requires us to keep our focus on Jesus and the massive scope of the gospel.

Remember, Jesus is worth more than comfort, and millions need to hear the gospel. The glory of God is at stake in all of this.

Be Content

Being content in this society is almost impossible. In fact, it's often seen as a weakness. And since there's big money to be made by those who can convince us that we need a new car or the latest gadget, this fight is massive.

The biblical idea of being content is being satisfied with God's reign and plan:

> Keep your life free from love of money, and be content with what you have, for he has said, "I will never leave you nor forsake you." (Hebrews 13:5)

This means that we don't have anxiety or fear because God is sovereign, his promises are firm, and he'll always be with us. Contentment is resting in God's purpose and care.

Sin means we're not satisfied or content with God's design. The first sin (Genesis 3) was a sin of discontent – wanting more. Rather than trusting in God's provision or wisdom or love, we can easily want independence and self-determination. Sin is the story of being discontent.

When we think about being content with what we have, we're often thinking about money or the things money can buy. As Christians it's easy to think we should simply strive to be happy in our current standard of living and not complain about it, right? But if being content isn't qualified, we can easily move down the wrong path. There's another critical element that's needed if we're to be biblical in our thinking about being content.

Being Content Is Not Enough

Even being content can be a "straw man" that helps us live for ourselves. Let me illustrate.

Let's say that a high-income couple has been living for their own pleasure. They relish a massive home, expensive cars, extravagant vacations, and only the best colleges for their children. Then one day, God grants them saving faith. And through hearing a sermon on being content, they recognize their materialistic longings and make an effort to be satisfied with what they have. They stop growing their expenses and even start giving money to their church.

Are they now an example of biblical contentment? No, they're still far away. They're still using most of their money for personal satisfaction and not for ministry.

Both the apostle Paul and the author of Hebrews found it important to include an additional element to contentment. Paul counseled our need for godliness, while the author of Hebrews stated that we must be free from the love of money.

But godliness with contentment is great gain. (1 Timothy 6:6)

Keep your life free from love of money, and be content with what you have, for he has said, "I will never leave you nor forsake you." (Hebrews 13:5)

In these verses being content doesn't simply stand on its own. Godliness means we adopt God's perspective on life and find purpose in living for the kingdom. We embrace God's values as our values, and God's mission as our mission. When we can live a life that focuses on bringing God glory in everything, and we're content in that, then we have it right.

In the Hebrews example (13:5), the author becomes very specific. Before contentment is what it should be, we need to get rid of our love for money. When we view money as belonging to God for the benefit of the kingdom, and we're happy with that, we have the right type of contentment. Another way of saying it is that we'll be thinking like stewards.

If our money priorities are wrong, we're not content with God's design and mission. Godly financial contentment is connected to being captured by the gospel and all that Jesus is for us.

Being content with our financial situation is important. But for this contentment to be God-honoring, it must come along with a godly disposition that longs to be fully committed to the glory of God. It needs to connect to living out the gospel in every aspect of life.

Contentment and Laziness

It's easy to think that being content has an element of laziness in it, or maybe a lack of determination or effort. But that's not the way it is for the Christian. In fact, when we align our heart with God's heart, we have an eternal purpose that we're to pursue with all the energy we have.

The Bible encourages us to live focused and energetic lives that pursue Jesus's mission until the end.

I do not account my life of any value nor as precious to myself, if only I may finish my course and the ministry that I received from the Lord Jesus, to testify to the gospel of the grace of God.(Acts 20:24)

Never be lacking in zeal, but keep your spiritual fervor, serving the Lord. (Romans 12:11 NIV)

Therefore, my beloved brothers, be steadfast, immovable, always abounding in the work of the Lord, knowing that in the Lord your labor is not in vain. (1 Corinthians 15:58)

The biblical idea of being content means we're satisfied with God's promises while working, with zeal, for the glory of Christ.

Contentment, then, is the product of a heart resting in God. It is the soul's enjoyment of that peace that passes all understanding. It is the outcome of my will being brought into subjection to the Divine will. It is the blessed assurance that God does all things well, and is, even now, making all things work together for my ultimate good.

– A. W. Pink –

Share Sacrificially

Generously helping those in need is a central element of life as a Christian. We're called to live by faith as we respond to the needs around us.

The righteous gives and does not hold back. (Proverbs 21:26)

Whoever has two tunics is to share with him who has none, and whoever has food is to do likewise. (Luke 3:11)

Sell your possessions, and give to the needy. Provide yourselves with moneybags that do not grow old, with a treasure in the heavens that does not fail, where no thief approaches and no moth destroys. (Luke 12:33)

Whoever sows sparingly will also reap sparingly, and whoever sows bountifully will also reap bountifully. (2 Corinthians 9:6)

Let the thief no longer steal, but rather let him labor, doing honest work with his own hands, so that he may have something to share with anyone in need. (Ephesians 4:28)

While these verses speak for themselves, Ephesians 4:28 struck me in a fresh way. A primary reason the thief should stop stealing and start working is so that has something to share. Therefore a primary motivation for working should be giving. Have you ever thought of that as a significant reason to work? It is in God's thinking.

James understood sharing as a critical component of true and living faith when he uses the sharing of possessions (James 2:14-17) as a foundational illustration for how faith without works is dead (2:14-26). For James, sharing is one way you show your faith.

Our willingness to share is often influenced by the other items in this section. Not loving money, being content with God's provision, and trusting God for the future are all needed in order to have a willingness to share as we should. The more important money is to me, the less likely I'll be inclined to share.

He who is not liberal with what he has does but deceive himself when he thinks he would be liberal if he had more.

– William Plumer –

Focus on the Gospel as We Give

As Paul encouraged the church of Corinth to give, he referenced the gospel – or at least part of the gospel – as the pivotal focus for them in their giving:

> For you know the grace of our Lord Jesus Christ, that though he was rich, yet for your sake he became poor, so that you by his poverty might become rich. (2 Corinthians 8:9)

In the incarnation, Jesus let go of indescribable splendor and became like us in order to save us. He immersed himself in this sinful world and all its brokenness so that he could be our substitute before God. He became poor so that we could be rich. In his poverty, we have eternal life.[9] Jesus's willingness to give himself should be our example in giving.

FOUR POSITIVE EXAMPLES

There are many helpful lessons we can learn from biblical characters interacting with money. Here are four worth thinking about:

Barnabas: Humble Stewardship

Barnabas was a humble, trustworthy risk-taker for the gospel. He seemed to understand what God was doing. When Saul (Paul) was converted, Barnabas saw the hand of God on him and went to his defense (Acts 9:26-27) even as everyone else hesitated.

In Acts 4, we see Barnabas making a bold financial decision for the kingdom:

> There was not a needy person among them, for as many as were owners of lands or houses sold them and brought the proceeds of what was sold and laid it at the apostles' feet, and it was distributed to each as any had need. Thus Joseph, who was also called by the apostles Barnabas (which means son of encouragement), a Levite, a native of Cyprus, sold a field that belonged to him and brought the money and laid it at the apostles' feet. (Acts 4:34-37)

As the Holy Spirit came upon the earliest believers, they *were of one heart and soul*. This deep unity and purpose affected how they thought about their personal wealth. Those who had wealth were using it to meet the needs of the church such that there wasn't a needy person there.

The unity of this early group of believers was much more than verbal agreement about the truths of the gospel. They were completely committed to each other. In these verses we see an example of what life should look like in the church. And what was Barnabas' role in this? He brought what God had given to him – money.

He sold a piece of land and simply gave the money to the apostles for the needs of the group. This is one way he and others who had wealth gave themselves to the gospel and to each other.

To be clear, there's no indication that these believers were forced to sell their property. And there's no indication that communal ownership was the rule of the day. Rather, the gospel simply created amazing perspective and purpose in these believers. And now they had the same radical, at-all-cost commitment to the kingdom that Jesus did.

What Barnabas did (and how he did it) was so exemplary that Luke contrasted it to the "gift" of Ananias and Sapphira in Acts 5:1-11. While Barnabas was concerned about the kingdom, Ananias and Sapphira had an evil, underlying motive. They saw an opportunity for personal benefit in their giving. And because of their evil motives and actions, God killed them both.

This passage is an amazing example of what a Holy Spirit-infused congregation should look like:

- It should be created by the Holy Spirit.
- It should be unified around Jesus and focused on the kingdom, with everything available to support God's purposes. When the Holy Spirit is working, believers give.[10]
- It should be holy in conduct. The Spirit's creation (this group of believers) was sacred – so sacred that Ananias and Sapphira both died because they attempted to bring an evil deception into a work God was doing.

This passage is about much more than giving to the church and taking care of those in need. We have a picture here of how the church should look: Spirit-filled, unified, and giving.

Can you imagine the impact that the church in North America (or anywhere, for that matter) would have if we absorbed the gospel the way these first-century Christians did? If we saw ourselves as stewards and not owners? Perhaps the persecuted church is growing in countries like China because there is a Spirit-saturated commitment that we do not.

Zacchaeus: The Money-Idol Is Replaced

> And behold, there was a man named Zacchaeus. He was a chief tax
> collector and was rich. And he was seeking to see who Jesus was, but
> on account of the crowd he could not, because he was small in stature.
> So he ran on ahead and climbed up into a sycamore tree to see him, for
> he was about to pass that way. And when Jesus came to the place, he
> looked up and said to him, "Zacchaeus, hurry and come down, for I must
> stay at your house today." So he hurried and came down and received
> him joyfully. And when they saw it, they all grumbled, "He has gone in
> to be the guest of a man who is a sinner." And Zacchaeus stood and said
> to the Lord, "Behold, Lord, the half of my goods I give to the poor. And
> if I have defrauded anyone of anything, I restore it fourfold." And Jesus
> said to him, "Today salvation has come to this house, since he also is a
> son of Abraham. For the Son of Man came to seek and to save the lost."
> (Luke 19:2-10)

Do you want to see a real miracle? Well, there's one in Luke 19!
We see salvation comes to someone who can more easily fit through
the eye of a needle than be saved. A spiritually dead, hardened, and
rich chief tax collector is given new life. Zacchaeus went from being
a self-serving, dishonest tool of Rome to a disciple controlled by a
new treasure.

When Zacchaeus experienced Jesus, something inside him
changed. In an instant, his reality was so altered that he did
something unimaginable. He gave away half of everything he had
and paid back fourfold those he had defrauded. After seeing this
change, Jesus publicly confirmed Zacchaeus's salvation.

Zacchaeus seems to be a living example of these words Jesus
spoke earlier:

> Any one of you who does not renounce all that he has cannot be my
> disciple. (Luke 14:33)

In the story which comes just before that of Zacchaeus, we see
the other possibility, which we looked at earlier (from Luke

18:18-30) – that of the rich and respected young man leading a "good" religious life, but who kept wealth as his god rather than embracing Jesus. With Zacchaeus, however, we see Jesus breaking the grip of idols.

God can do the impossible and rescue anyone – the worst of us. Faith in Jesus means the heart has been changed and is open to kingdom thinking and priorities. And idols lose their grip.

What's the real point of Zacchaeus's story? While all this is to lead us to Jesus, the comparison of Zacchaeus to the rich young ruler should give us pause. These two stories are very much about the here-and-now impact Jesus has on those who believe. This is about the reorientation Jesus brings to life. This story, and all the difficult and wonderful teachings of Jesus, should lead us to examine our lives. Has Jesus replaced our idols? What excuses are we using as we hang on to the attractions of this world?

This salvation encounter was no accident, and Zacchaeus's conversion – or anyone's conversion for that matter – is just as miraculous as the parting of the Red Sea or the raising of Lazarus from the dead.

One other thing worth considering. Luke emphasizes joy and happiness and excitement when it comes to belief (see 1:14; 8:13; 10:17; 13:17; 15:5, 9, 32; 19:6, 37). We see it here as well:

> And when Jesus came to the place, he looked up and said to him, "Zacchaeus, hurry and come down, for I must stay at your house today." So he hurried and came down and received him *joyfully*. (Luke 19:5-6)

Zacchaeus didn't let go of his wealth grudgingly. He did it joyfully, because earthly wealth lost its value when compared to the value of real treasure.

The cheerful givers God loves (2 Corinthians 9:7) are those who give because Jesus is their joy.

The Poor Widow: Knowing God

True followers of God look like the widow we meet in Luke 21. She had almost nothing, and her earthly needs were real, and her faith was deep. And so she gave. There was no fanfare, and the amount of her offering was extremely small.

> Jesus looked up and saw the rich putting their gifts into the offering box, and he saw a poor widow put in two small copper coins. And he said, "Truly, I tell you, this poor widow has put in more than all of them. For they all contributed out of their abundance, but she out of her poverty put in all she had to live on." (Luke 21:1-4)

Jesus saw this widow as one who gave more than the rich folks. Why? Because she saw God rightly, and she responded rightly. True disciples give because God is worthy and they've abandoned their lives to the One who cares for them. They don't have a tight grip on money, and worldly acclaim means nothing – God is their reality.

Here in Luke (as well as with Mark's parallel account in 21:1-4), this story of the widow's offering is preceded by a warning to beware of religious teachers (scribes) who call attention to their piety and status, even while possessing neither true piety nor status in God's kingdom. There's a great contrast between these self-elevated, it's-all-about-the-show teachers and this poor widow. For the scribes, it was about position and power and being noticed. For the humble widow, life was about God. The scribes and this widow lived in different realities, both here and in the life to come.

In *Habits of Grace*, David Mathis writes this:

Do you ever abstain from something you'd otherwise think of as "the needs of life" in order to give to others? Nothing shows our hearts like sacrifice. When we're willing to not only give from our excess but embrace personal loss or disadvantage for the sake of showing generosity toward others, we say loudly and clearly—even if only to our own souls—that we have a greater love than ourselves and our comforts.[11]

Among the many things this story can teach are:

- Being cherished by God is different from being acclaimed by this world.

- The size of the gift is important to the world, but the size of our God is important to the faithful.

- Great faith produces "crazy" God-pleasing action that doesn't need to be acknowledged by the world.

This widow's story leaves me in awe. As I ponder her act, I really struggle. It feels like I'm missing something. What exactly is the point here? I'm glad to learn about humility and giving, but I'm sure there's much more. I know that this woman will continually speak to me. If God is everything to me, should I be following her example? This is so "out there" that my defenses kick in.

I'm not sure what to make of it except that this woman knew God. It seems that her existence was so entwined with God's that she saw things clearly while the religious leaders had no clue. She knew who God was and what really mattered. She entrusted all she was and had to him.

Charity is, indeed, a great thing, and a gift of God, and when it is rightly ordered likens us to God Himself, as far as that is possible; for it is charity which makes the man.

– John Chrysostom –

Jesus: Rejecting Earthly Wealth for Eternal Gain

Jesus was not immune to the temptation of wealth and power:

> And the devil took him up and showed him all the kingdoms of the world in a moment of time, and said to him, "To you I will give all this authority and their glory, for it has been delivered to me, and I give it to whom I will. If you, then, will worship me, it will all be yours." And Jesus answered him, "It is written, 'You shall worship the Lord your God, and him only shall you serve.'" (Luke 4:5-8)

After fasting for forty days and being weak and hungry, Jesus faced the devil and his three temptations. These temptations were undoubtedly the devil's best chance at defeating Jesus in his vulnerable condition. One of these temptations promised him all the kingdoms of the world.

Here's where it gets interesting. The devil promised abundant earthly wealth and power and pleasure. But if Jesus gave in, he would lose the eternal reign that would be his through the pain of the cross. Thankfully, he stood firm and trusted his Father to be faithful in all he had promised. Jesus was steadfast in giving himself to God's glory and the joy to come.

We, too, face a test of faith. In receiving the gospel, we admit our sin and its fatality. We acknowledge that we need saving because we've rejected God and gone our own way. In essence, we agree that embracing this world and its priorities leads to death, while embracing Jesus – and all he accomplished for us on the cross – leads to life.

It's important that the promises of God in Christ mean more to us than what this world offers. It's important that we have our eyes firmly fixed on Jesus as our savior and the One we follow. This is not easy but the rewards are eternal:

The kingdom of heaven is like treasure hidden in a field, which a man found and covered up. Then in his joy he goes and sells all that he has and buys that field. (Matthew 13:44)

All that Jesus is for us should make everything else lose its value and compel us to use everything – including our money – to bring glory to God.

Do not love the world or the things in the world. If anyone loves the world, the love of the Father is not in him. For all that is in the world— the desires of the flesh and the desires of the eyes and pride of life— is not from the Father but is from the world. And the world is passing away along with its desires, but whoever does the will of God abides forever. (1 John 2:15-17)

APPLICATION

Before moving on, answer the following application questions. Also, review and complete the "Financial Assessment Report" in the appendix at the end of this book. This should take only a couple of minutes.

1. In what ways do you struggle with stewardship?

2. What warning or instruction do you need to focus on?

3. What character example was interesting to you and why?

3

Be Aware of the Struggles

Knowing and Conquering Our Weaknesses

Step three to winning the money battle is recognizing and knowing the struggles that will come our way as we think about our financial planning from a gospel-saturated core. Because fighting sin is a lifelong effort and our worldly inclinations don't simply disappear, we must know our enemy. In the power of the Holy Spirit, we must go to war:

> For we do not wrestle against flesh and blood, but against the rulers, against the authorities, against the cosmic powers over this present darkness, against the spiritual forces of evil in the heavenly places. (Ephesians 6:12)

The Christian walks a narrow path that leads away from the inclinations of the world we live in. Belief in Jesus is the first step down that path. Through the kindness of God and a Spirit-changed heart, we see the truth and believe that Jesus, through his cross-work, makes us right with God. Then the reality of this seismic change works its way into every aspect of life as we absorb God's word.

As a disciple, moving down the narrow path is a difficult and violent journey. As we fight, works of the flesh are put to death as

Jesus proves himself to us in every area of life. This is a war that will certainly contain serious battles over money.

Let's look at some of the struggles we face:

WALKING BY FAITH

Paul reminds us that "we walk by faith, not by sight" (2 Corinthians 5:7).[12] Walking by faith is not for the faint-hearted. But it is for those who are children of God.

Walking by faith means that in our everyday moments and decisions, instead of simply following the path of least resistance, we believe everything that Jesus is for us, and we act accordingly. We follow God's wisdom for us and trust him for the outcome. The reality of this is that walking by faith means moving against the wisdom of this world. This will mean that the world will view us as fools.

> Let no one deceive himself. If anyone among you thinks that he is wise in this age, let him become a fool that he may become wise. (1 Corinthians 3:18)

The primary example of how we are "fools" in this world is found in our belief in and dependence on Jesus (1 Corinthians 1:18-29). We trust that our only hope of being reconciled to God is Jesus and his saving work. Because we're depending on Jesus and not on ourselves, our lives are turned upside down. We entrust ourselves to God knowing that we have new citizenship in a kingdom where he reigns.

A Jesus-dependent, faith-driven life is not compatible with earthly wisdom. Earthly wisdom leads us away from the gospel and fosters thinking that bends, ignores, and rejects the truth.

In 1 Corinthians 3:18-19, we see an example of earthly wisdom. The Christians in Corinth were aligning themselves with individual teachers of the gospel such as Paul or Apollos. And because worldly wisdom can lead to a focus on the messenger rather than on God, the Corinthian believers were not unified. Here was an example of how we can lose our unity when we move our focus away from the gospel.

Many others in Scripture give us examples of walking by faith. Noah, living in the middle of an unbelieving and hostile society, listened to God rather than man:

> By faith Noah, being warned by God concerning events as yet unseen, in reverent fear constructed an ark for the saving of his household. By this he condemned the world and became an heir of the righteousness that comes by faith. (Hebrews 11:7)

Daniel's focus on God moved him to ignore the decree that made his faithful allegiance to God illegal:

> When Daniel knew that the document had been signed, he went to his house where he had windows in his upper chamber open toward Jerusalem. He got down on his knees three times a day and prayed and gave thanks before his God, as he had done previously. (Daniel 6:10)

After being told of the hostile opposition awaiting him, Paul said:

> I am ready not only to be imprisoned but even to die in Jerusalem for the name of the Lord Jesus. (Acts 21:13)

This is walking by faith.

If we're not careful, earthly wisdom will carry the day when we think about money and all the things money can buy. We need to be aware of how earthly wisdom can press us into compromise. It's easy to get caught up in this world's priorities and neglect the most important realities. We need to step back and question retirement, insurance, college, leisure, debt, investment strategy, housing, transportation – everything. It's easy to simply adopt a perspective that has nothing to do with God's glory and everything to do with following the societal path.

Blessed is the man who walks not in the counsel of the wicked, nor stands in the way of sinners, nor sits in the seat of scoffers. (Psalm 1:1)

If our aim is to walk by faith in the area of personal finances, we must know that it will not be life as usual. God calls us to live lives that focus on exalting Jesus.

It is better to fail in an attempt to exercise faith than to let it lie dormant and fruitless. God never belittles those who attempt to follow Him, but He does chasten those who refuse to attempt anything for Him.

– Kent Hughes –

PRIORITIES, NOT GOALS

I'd like to mention a critically important reality that drives our financial planning. It's our priorities – the pursuit of what's important to us.

I intentionally use the word *priorities* here rather than *goals*. It's more accurate and honest. Because we have a limited amount of money and must evaluate and reevaluate how to allocate our resources, it's our priorities that we actually fund.

For where your treasure is, there will your heart be also. (Luke 12:34)

In my thirty-five-plus years of working with hundreds and speaking to thousands, I've had the opportunity to hear about many decision-driving priorities. A few years ago, I met a man who helps people create the needed resources so they can be frozen when they die (cryonic preservation). It's a priority that takes massive amounts of money.

I once talked with a couple living in a filthy, run-down shoebox of a house, though they had much more money than they would ever spend. I've talked with families who've struggled for years because their resources are going toward the care of a special needs child. And I've talked with successful high-income professionals so deep in debt they could barely pay their bills. It doesn't take long to see that our priorities dictate how we use money.

We allocate our resources to the things most important to us. When you buy a house or a television or a car, or when you spend money on a vacation or a night out, or when you borrow money for college or put money away for retirement or give money to your church, it always reflects your priorities and values.

Even decisions that are seemingly forced on us can reflect our priorities. For example, someone might say, "Because my car broke down and I needed $3,000 for repairs, I had no choice but to borrow the money to pay for this. And now the payments on this loan really messed up my budget and caused me to..." We might wonder why there was no reserve to handle this likely problem? If the answer is "I can't afford to create a reserve," we should really ask, "Why not? Can you afford to pay off the debt you just created? If you have the money to pay off the debt, didn't you have the money to fund a reserve?" It may be that inappropriate spending decisions left this person with little ability to reserve for the unexpected.

YOUR UNIQUE PATH

A life captured by Jesus will be radical and lived out on the unique path of God's design. This unique and faith-building path is designed to demonstrate the value of Jesus. It can often seem very lonely if we're not focused on him.

Peter's Unique Path

One morning after Jesus's resurrection, he gave Peter a glimpse of what was coming (John 21:18-22). He said that crucifixion was in Peter's future too.

Can you imagine how Peter's mind must have been spinning? What do you do with something like that? Peter had just experienced the horror of Jesus's crucifixion, and now it was coming for him too?

In his search for understanding, Peter asked Jesus if John would suffer in the same way. Jesus's response was pointed: "Don't worry about my plans for John; you follow me" (my paraphrase).

While we probably won't face crucifixion, it's easy to look around to see if we're being treated "fairly" or if others are living like we're living. God loves his children and has promised to care for us. We're called to trust him with our lives and to live on mission.

Paul's Unique Path

Paul's unique path gave him a lonely experience when, after faithfully preaching the gospel and ministering to the flock, no one showed up to stand with him when he went to "trial." But God was with him.

> At my first defense no one came to stand by me, but all deserted me. May it not be charged against them! But the Lord stood by me and strengthened me. (2 Timothy 4:16-17)

Following Jesus means a path of focused dedication to him in all we do. It means a life of soul-satisfying mission.[13] And there's no doubt that faithfully dealing with our finances is a part of the journey.

But just like Peter, we can be tempted to look around to see if the path ahead is easy or difficult, or what everyone else is doing. It's easy to take our eyes off Jesus rather than to trust him and follow. The easier path can be tempting because it doesn't require faith. For the Christian, however, it should always be "more of Jesus and less of me." Remember, Jesus cares for us, and his yoke is easy and his burden is light.[14]

While I'm grateful for the many Christians in my life who treasure Jesus, who can pray for me, and who can show me what a faithful life looks like, they can't be faithful for me. If I'm to follow the path God has for me, I, just like Peter and Paul, must give myself to God and his sufficiency, through the power of the Holy Spirit.

So what difficult thing is God calling you to do? Get rid of your debt? Spend less on comfort or pleasure? Give more? Go into full-time Christian service? Adopt a child?

Remember, the path God has for you is for you. In faith and obedience, through the power of the Holy Spirit, we're called to look to Jesus and follow. Being a true steward of God's resources puts us on a difficult, self-denying path that can, at times, feel lonely. But Jesus is with us, and the treasure that's before us is beyond description.

HANDLING MONEY IS NOT ABOUT MONEY

Every Christian parent wants their child to do more than simply follow the rules. We want to see a heart that, because of the gospel, is longing to follow Jesus. Not from fear-driven duty, but from love and a Christ-exalting vision for life that comes with believing the gospel.

In the same way, the best way to follow Jesus in our financial affairs is not out of duty, but rather from a heart that wants what God wants, a heart that stays near to him, and not like what Jesus described about so many in his day: "This people honors me with their lips, but their heart is far from me" (Matthew 15:8).[15]

It's easy for a Christian discussion about money to completely miss the main point – being faithful to Jesus. We can talk about financial tactics and clean up our debt and reduce our expenses and even give more, and yet be missing God's heart and vision for us.

Money is neutral. It's not good or bad. It's currency. So when the discussion is focused on money, it's easy to keep the spiritual issues at a distance. By simply talking about money, we can reduce the likelihood that we'll need to confront our idols. We can feign spirituality while actually keeping the Spirit at bay. Talking about money often ends up being strategic or informational or educational without really changing us.

Through the gospel, however, we experience the necessary heart-change in order to think about money rightly. If we really want to bring correct change to our lives, and if we truly want a gospel-saturated approach to everything – including our finances – we need to focus on the beauty and magnitude of Jesus and his saving work for us and a response that reflects God's kindness.

The best result of a gospel-saturated discussion about money is not simply a change in our spending or saving or giving, but also a Spirit-infused change of heart. I'm praying that the Spirit will help us see Jesus clearly, and that in turn, we'll long to follow him in every way, with joy and zeal.

Sadly, while many are interested in a discussion about money, most seem to be interested in the less important issues like how to invest, how to create a bigger retirement account, or how to save taxes or pay for college. Most aren't as enthusiastic about discussing money in light of the gospel.

FIGHTING THE PROSPERITY GOSPEL

The prosperity gospel is a belief that God would have his children experience financial prosperity. In a positive sense, this means that God's design is to bless his children, here and now, with significant financial benefits. Another way to say this might be: if we live out God's design for us, and if we're in the center of his will (whatever that means), we can expect financial success that isn't normal. In a negative sense, it's an expectation that Christians will not – or should not – experience the financial hardship that others might.

But the prosperity gospel misses the key thrust found in these words of Jesus:

> Do not lay up for yourselves treasures on earth, where moth and rust destroy and where thieves break in and steal, but lay up for yourselves treasures in heaven, where neither moth nor rust destroys and where thieves do not break in and steal. For where your treasure is, there your heart will be also. (Matthew 6:19-21)

The Here-and-Now Benefits of the Gospel

To be sure, there are amazing life-is-made-better benefits of believing the gospel and being united with Christ. And these benefits are ours because Jesus is ours here and now. The Christian should have a life that knows God's love in a deep and intimate way. This life should overflow with peace and hope and joy and purpose.

We shouldn't be captured by the soul-sucking entrapments of this world or be anxious about anything.

The Christian's self-sacrificing love for others should create a noticeable Christ-exalting reputation that glorifies God and communicates hope in Jesus. Life should be fulfilling and meaningful and victorious because we serve the living and eternal King who saved us and will never leave us.

Because Jesus frees us from sin's slavery, the grip that idols would have over us is broken. We can rest knowing that God is enough, and we can joyfully engage with those around us. Our situation – whatever it is – always works for our good, because God is for us.

Proverbs 3:6 is absolutely true in its instruction about trusting the Lord: "In all your ways acknowledge him, and he will make straight your paths." The path of life, for the Christian, should be different, because we can let go of self and focus on the One who controls what comes into our lives. We should be hope-filled instead of fearful, content rather than complaining, thankful instead of whining, prayerful instead of self-reliant, and steadfast in the middle of chaos. Our path should be straight and full of joy because Jesus cares for us. Indeed, life should be much better here because we have Jesus.

A Worldly Emphasis

The prosperity gospel, however, embraces a worldly vision of what life should look like for the Christian. It pushes God's design for us – living out God's goodness as Jesus did – into the corner, and it replaces that with greed and idols. Instead of striving for a self-sacrificing, love-at-all-cost, live-by-faith, everything-belongs-to-God life, the expectation for us includes material wealth.

The prosperity gospel ignores Jesus's example and his instruction to embrace a humble, self-sacrificing life. And, it ignores countless numbers of faithful Christians who have lived steadfast, Christ-exalting lives while absorbing all the pain and rejection and poverty this world can dish out (Matthew 5:11; 10:22, 39; 19:29; Acts 5:41; 9:16; Romans 8:17; 2 Corinthians 1:7; 4:11; 12:10; Philippians 1:29; 3:10; Hebrews 11:25; James 5:10; 1 Peter 3:14; 4:16; 5:10). Instead, the prosperity gospel seems to follow the desires of Simon (Acts 8) who thought that the gospel was the key to worldly success.

God's design for us is to find sufficiency in Jesus as the world wages its war of pain and destruction, and as we pursue the Christ-exalting, others-oriented, walk-by-faith mission that we're on. We aren't exempt from struggle; we're here to showcase victory in the struggle.

We All Struggle with This

We're all susceptible to various forms of the prosperity gospel. We can see it in the temptation to question God's love for us when things don't go as we'd like. It's a struggle because we don't, or won't, embrace God's design – to find our sufficiency in Jesus and approach life as he did:

> Whoever would be great among you must be your servant, and whoever would be first among you must be your slave, even as the Son of Man came not to be served but to serve, and to give his life as a ransom for many. (Matthew 20:26-28)

> Have this mind among yourselves, which is yours in Christ Jesus, who, though he was in the form of God, did not count equality with God a thing to be grasped, but emptied himself, by taking the form of a servant, being born in the likeness of men. And being found in human form, he humbled himself by becoming obedient to the point of death, even death on a cross. (Philippians 2:5-8)

If we're focused on this world, it's natural to think that the God who owns everything and wants his children happy would also want his children to have lots of money. We struggle to believe that life in the palm of God's hand could include lifelong illness, the loss of a child or spouse, or poverty. From birth until death we're bombarded with the idea that being fulfilled must include the things of this world. It's easy to buy into the wrong vision.

As Christians, when we critically question the sickness, pain, and tragedy in our life or in the lives of those we care about, or when we don't get the answer we want from fervent prayer, or when we lose a job, or our marriage isn't what we'd hoped for, then at some level we're saying, "I deserve better." This is prosperity thinking. Instead of believing that God's sovereign action in my life is always good and his grace is always sufficient, it's easy to doubt that God exists or that he cares for me.

Maybe you have a dream you just can't give up. Not a Christ-exalting, kingdom-advancing dream, but a self-centered, controlling, this-would-make-my-life-great dream. The words *new* and *better* are often a part of this (a new car, a new house, a new spouse, better vacations, a better job, etc.). Through the power of the Holy Spirit we can embrace Jesus instead of worldly ambitions and idols, and seek to be joyfully content as we pursue life in Christ.

What Does Faith Really Produce?

The prosperity gospel has one thing right. Faith in Jesus does produce massive change. But the wealth that we gain is *real* wealth – Jesus himself.

The problem with the prosperity gospel is that the desires are too low. It embraces financial comfort here rather than eternal beauty and satisfaction in Jesus forever. We're new people with new aspirations and new hope and a new willingness to give our lives to the kingdom. We have true riches that will never vanish.

When it comes to money and what money can buy, we must fight to know that the victory God has for us here doesn't necessarily mean financial prosperity. And if it does, we're stewards and not owners.

FEAR

In my first "Money and the Gospel" class, I had a real awakening when we talked about fear and money. I didn't anticipate the sudden emotional surge that would come with that topic. There was real sobbing because of the fear that leads to depending on money instead of God. Money had become the one thing that could alleviate the fear of want. Not God, but money.

Fear is a gripping panic that comes with an understanding that we're helpless in the face of pain or struggle. For the Christian, fear tells us that we're not thinking or believing the way we should.

In Matthew 8 we find a story of fear and faith. The disciples were in a boat with Jesus while a storm raged around them. Assuming death was imminent, and with Jesus asleep, they were controlled by earthly fear. In its grip, they woke Jesus and said, "Save us, Lord; we are perishing."

Here's where it gets interesting. Jesus responded, "Why are you afraid, O you of little faith?" Then He calmed the storm.

It's easy to think that Jesus was unreasonable in his rebuke. After all, who wouldn't be afraid in that situation? Who wouldn't be in a panic? Did Jesus really think the disciples shouldn't fear?

Well, yes. If God is in control and cares about his children, and if he promises to be everything we need in every situation, we don't need to be afraid. God will see us through everything he brings our way, and we'll emerge more like Jesus. If that means death, our face-to-face life with Jesus begins. Why should we fear?

Jesus believed that trusting God conquers fear. Believing that God is faithful and will never leave us means we don't need to be afraid:

When I am afraid, I put my trust in you. (Psalm 56:3)

At what point are *you* captured by fear? At what point does faith in the sovereign hand of God fall under the weight of events and circumstances he brings your way?

A robust faith will trust God in everything.

I find it interesting that on the one hand we've made the massive commitment to entrust our souls to God through the work of Jesus on the cross, while on the other hand we may not trust him when daily life closes in on us. The circumstances and difficulties of this life can become more important than the welfare of our eternal souls. That seems upside down, right?

Jesus's point in the boat was this: live or die, God is enough.

Faith-filled, Spirit-guided prayer to the God who cares about his children should take the place of fear (Philippians 4:6; 1 Peter 5:7). We're called to live out the reality that all events owe their existence to a sovereign God who is with us through ease or difficulty.

Fear and Money

It may be that fear drives our financial decisions. We save more than we should because we're afraid of a lean retirement. We spend too much on college because we're afraid our children won't have elevated earnings or social status. We buy the expensive car because we're afraid the world won't see us as being successful. We spend more than we should on ourselves because we're afraid we'll miss out on our self-centered dreams.

Fear and greed can produce results that look the same. We may think someone who piles up resources is simply greedy. It could be, however, that fear is in control.

It's easy to think that fear is a helpful emotion and can create the energy we need to work for the necessities of life. But this is not God's way. Faith is God's answer. Fear says, "God is not sovereign in the things that come my way. He's not in this situation, and it's up to me to figure it out." Faith says, "God is in control and cares for me and is always working for my good. I have nothing to fear, because he will never leave me and he will give me what I need, so I must focus on being faithful."

In difficulty, faith turns to prayer:

I sought the LORD, and he answered me and delivered me from all my fears. (Psalm 34:4)

Thinking about Fear Differently

In his book *Things Not Seen*, Jon Bloom says this:

Fear is a call to exercise faith. So we can stop dreading fear. Instead, we can see fear as another means God is using to fulfill his promise to complete the good work he began in us.[16]

Instead of simply being afraid and trying not to be afraid, we should recognize fear as the symptom of a deeper issue. In many ways fear and faith are opposites (Psalm 56:3). When we're afraid, faith in God and in all that Jesus is for us is in the back seat, and we're not believing the truth.

Here are four steps we might take when we're afraid:

1. Pray (Psalm 34:4; Philippians 4:6-7).

2. Know that God is with you (Isaiah 41:10; Psalms 23:4; 118:6-7) and that fear is not from God (2 Timothy 1:7).

3. Examine yourself for pride. You may be thinking you deserve something better. Humble yourself (1 Peter 5:6-7).

4. Know that there's reward in the struggle (1 Peter 3:14).

Therefore I tell you, do not be anxious about your life, what you will eat, nor about your body, what you will put on. For life is more than food, and the body more than clothing. Consider the ravens: they neither sow nor reap, they have neither storehouse nor barn, and yet God feeds them. Of how much more value are you than the birds! And which of you by being anxious can add a single hour to his span of life? If then you are not able to do as small a thing as that, why are you anxious about the rest? (Luke 12:22-26)

For God gave us a spirit not of fear but of power and love and self-control. (2 Timothy 1:7)

Fear and Greed have much in common. Both fail to grasp the magnitude of God. Both refuse to rest in God's sovereign plan and promises.

Interestingly, the one who is greedy is often seen as a horrible, shameful person, while we're empathetic to the poor soul living in fear. In truth, both exhibit a faithlessness that doesn't grasp the faithfulness of God.

If we allow money to become our master, it will lead to fear of loss... money will never relent in its pursuit of everything we have
— Ivan Mesa[17] —

GREED AND COVETOUSNESS

Greed is a sinful, self-centered desire to have something (money, time, toys, your neighbor's wife, etc.) for our own purposes or to have more than we should. Greed and a God-dependent, content life are enemies. For the Christian, greed must die, or the reality of one's salvation should be in doubt:

> For you may be sure of this, that everyone who is sexually immoral or impure, or who is covetous (that is, an idolater), has no inheritance in the kingdom of Christ and God. (Ephesians 5:5)

When we have a desire to be rich, money is our idol, Jesus is not our Lord, and our soul is in danger:

> Those who desire to be rich fall into temptation, into a snare, into many senseless and harmful desires that plunge people into ruin and destruction. For the love of money is a root of all kinds of evils. It is through this craving that some have wandered away from the faith and pierced themselves with many pangs. But as for you, O man of God, flee these things. Pursue righteousness, godliness, faith, love, steadfastness, gentleness. (1 Timothy 6:9-11)

This passage in 1 Timothy puts the pursuit of wealth in opposition to the pursuit of righteousness, godliness, faith, love, a steadfast Christian life, and gentleness. In other words, we can't do both. To pursue wealth is to move away from godly character.

The pursuit of wealth works against the truth that sin was conquered on the cross. Greed fights against the natural outcome of the Spirit's presence in the believer, which is a growing, Christlike character.[18]

If it's prudent to build an emergency reserve or save for retirement, how do I know if greed is my motive? There are times when greed is obvious to everyone, even the greedy person. Often, however, it's not that obvious. And since greed is a matter of the heart, it's messy.

One thing's for sure: the person living in the clutches of greed is not grasping the gospel as the overwhelming treasure that it is.

So how do I know if I'm greedy?

Sometimes, if we're being honest, we know. It's a matter of confession and repentance. Here are five things you might do to search your heart in this matter:

1. Question yourself. Am I in the Word? Does the gospel and the call to spread the gospel consume me? Is the glory of Christ my life's pursuit? If not, our motives are questionable.

2. Invite a godly person to ask you the difficult personal questions about your financial priorities:

– How much debt do you have? What's the character (home, credit card, auto, etc.) of your debt?

– How much are you giving away?

– How much are you spending on lifestyle extras? Why?

– What changes should you make? How will you do that?

3. Measure yourself against helpful standards. For example:

– Are you saving more in your retirement plan than you're giving away? (I use this question as a control in my life. It helps me keep first things first. At a minimum, I will not put my retirement before funding the spread of the gospel.)

– Do you have a lifestyle that's self-focused, or are you living for the kingdom? How is this evident?

4. Prayerfully study these passages: Luke 12:13-21; Ephesians 5:3; Galatians 5:16-18, 5:24.

5. Pray for the Spirit to reveal greed to you, and pray for the faith to take action against it.

The real problem is our tendency to settle for the inferior treasures of this world instead of the treasure of infinite value – Jesus himself. David Mathis makes a great statement about greed and the gospel:

> *The one who possessed everything made himself nothing that we might have everything in him... "Though he was rich, yet for your sake he became poor, so that you by his poverty might become rich" (2 Corinthians 8:9)... [Jesus] rose again over greed, death, and hell, and is preparing, for those whom he possesses, a new creation in which they will own it all. (1 Corinthians 3:21; Matthew 5:5)[19]*

PLANNING FOR RETIREMENT

What do you think retirement looks like for a faith-filled Christian who's consumed by the gospel? How does someone in their sixties, seventies, eighties, or nineties function when the Holy Spirit has been increasing their faith and creating in them an ever-increasing love for and commitment to Jesus? Does it look like sitting in a fishing boat all day?

- Moses was in his eighties when he approached Pharaoh (Exodus 7:7).

- While it's difficult to be sure, the prophet Daniel may have been in his seventies or eighties when he was thrown into the lion's den.

- The apostle John was probably writing Scripture in his seventies or eighties.

And here's what Paul could say about his life, all the way to its end:

> I have fought the good fight, I have finished the race, I have kept the faith. (2 Timothy 4:7)

We need to be careful when we think about retirement. The rich fool in Luke 12:13-16 was condemned for the way he thought about it. His goal was to relax, not worry about the expenses, and spend his remaining years selfishly enjoying life. Earthly wealth was his, but he was bankrupt when it came to eternal wealth. His effort was focused on the temporary.

A common response to this parable is: "I don't want to be like this foolish man, so I will serve God diligently *and* build as much wealth as I can." But this response misses the point of the parable. The foolish man was using his energy and resources to fund something that was temporary and small compared to all that could have been his: eternal joy in the presence of God.

This story brings the whole concept of retirement into question. The foolish man aimed toward a day when he could stop working and have a carefree, all-expenses-paid, live-for-myself life. The vision of retirement that we pursue dictates how we use valuable resources, and it exposes the disposition of our heart.

We should all be working to spread the gospel and to be ministers of the gospel to the end. Does this sound radical? It should be the natural result of a life turned upside down by Jesus.

As Paul saw his end coming, his declaration was, "I have fought the good fight, I have finished the race, I have kept the faith." Surely his ambition was to work for the kingdom until the end.

While it's simplistic to say that worship is love,
it's a fact that what we love most
will determine what we genuinely worship.

– Bob Kauflin –

APPLICATION

1. How is walking by faith in your financial decisions difficult?

2. How might fear or greed influence your money decisions?

3. What do you hope for in "retirement"?

4

Face Real Questions

Answers to Fill in the Gaps

Even if our hearts are right, our joy is full, and the destination is clear, there can be difficult questions about winning the money battle. Step four is an attempt to answer a few of these questions.

I've found that the questions addressed in this chapter are common. But please know that while I'm giving you my thoughts in response, they're no substitute for the wisdom that comes from God:

> If any of you lacks wisdom, let him ask God, who gives generously to all without reproach, and it will be given him. (James 1:5)

IS TITHING A NEW TESTAMENT RULE?

On the topic of tithing, let me start with an overview of what I believe to be biblical. Three things:

1. All that we are and everything God has entrusted to us belongs to Him. We are stewards.

2. God's kindness toward us in Jesus, and all that this means, should consume us and be the heartbeat of every aspect of our lives.

3. We should live in a way that brings glory to God.

The exact question we're asking here is important. To ask, "How much of my income *must* I give to the church, missions, the poor, and other ministry needs?" is inappropriate. We should know, with joy, that our lives don't belong to us, and neither does the money in our retirement accounts. We should joyfully be driven by God's agenda – his glory in our sanctification and in the proclamation of the gospel. Our goal should be to place everything we are and everything we have at Jesus's feet.

So let me list four problems with using the tithe as the obligatory standard:

1. Since Jesus, the perfect High Priest, has replaced the Old Testament priesthood, the tithe is no longer needed or advocated in the New Testament. When the tithe is mentioned, it's connected to Jesus's scathing rebuke of the Pharisees (Matthew 23) or to amplify the status of Melchizedek (Hebrews 7).

2. When Paul emphasizes the need for giving, he doesn't talk in terms of the tithe. Instead, he urges Christians to give as God has prospered them (1 Corinthians 16:1-2) and he wants to make sure they know three things about giving (2 Corinthians 9:7):

   —Generous giving means generous blessing.

   —They should give after thoughtful consideration and not because of coercion.

   —Giving should be done with joyful hearts.

3. While for most, tithing would mean giving more than they do now, for some the tithe can become a giving maximum. So once the 10 percent goal is achieved and their duty is done, the 90 percent belongs to them. So the tithe as an obligation is considered either the minimum or the

maximum. For some, therefore, tithing is oppressive; for others it's a ridiculously small amount.

4. There is a better way. Not obligation but shared vision. Through the presence of the Holy Spirit, Christians share God's vision for the outcome of their salvation, bringing glory to God in all of life.

Rule-making often reduces our ability to function as God intends – in Spirit-led freedom. I'm not saying that we should give 100 percent of our income to church and missions. I'm saying that 100 percent of everything we have is important. It all belongs to God.

The financial decisions we make should be made prayerfully. The house we buy, the car we own, the food we eat, the clothes we buy, and the way we think about college costs, vacations, and retirement are all very important because the glory of God is involved.

The question "How much *must* I give?" is out of place for the Christian. Hopefully, we're praying, "God, make me aware of the value of the gospel, and help me glorify you in every financial decision I make. Help me be a good steward of your gifts."

HOW SHOULD I THINK ABOUT GIVING?

Just as it's common to ask how much we *must* give, it's also common to think that biblical giving is all about the amount. This couldn't be further from the truth. Biblical giving revolves around the way my heart is aligned with God's heart (again, see Matthew 15:8). Giving is what happens when we live out our salvation.

But it's also true that if we understand the gospel the way we should, our giving – at least for most – o will increase. Why?

Because we'll see the gospel as the singularly most important, infinitely valuable, everyone-must-hear, news that exists. And we'll want to put our time and resources into pursuing God's agenda: saving the lost and maturing the saints.

Following are four foundational beliefs that combine to shape the heart for giving.

1. The Gospel Is Our Treasure

In a short parable in Matthew 13:44, Jesus created a contrast between the value of God's reign and the value of everything else:

> The kingdom of heaven is like treasure hidden in a field, which a man found and covered up. Then in his joy he goes and sells all that he has and buys that field.

Not only does this man sell everything to possess the field and its treasure, he does it with joy. He's totally committed to what's most valuable.

Being captured by the grace of God through the cross-work of Jesus opens our eyes to the infinite value of the gospel and the lesser value of those things that would compete for our loyalty.

It's impossible to give as we should if our money, or the things money can buy, are as valuable to us as the gospel. All that Jesus is for us should dominate our focus and serve as the controlling influence in our lives.

When Jesus is our treasure, money is not.

2. We're Here for the Mission

It's tempting to think that the Christian life is simply a better and "cleaner" version of what the world offers. But that's not true. Our world is not just improved; it's a new reality where Jesus rules over everything, sin has been defeated, and life takes on an eternal scope.

Just like Jesus, we're here to live fully for the glory of God:

Whether you eat or drink, or whatever you do, do all to the glory of God. (1 Corinthians 10:31)

Our mission – to bring God glory – should dominate the way we raise our children, do our work, spend our leisure time, and manage our money.

We're new people with a new reality that doesn't conform to this world. We're here as disciples. We're here to follow Jesus in his mission.

Jesus told his disciples, "If anyone would come after me, let him deny himself and take up his cross and follow me." (Matthew 16:24)

If anyone serves me, he must follow me; and where I am, there will my servant be also. If anyone serves me, the Father will honor him. (John 12:26)

So we not only possess a treasure of infinite value; our lives now are meant to show the world how valuable our treasure really is. When we embrace Jesus as we should and live for the mission, giving becomes natural.

3. Being Like Jesus Means Giving

Jesus was all about giving. It was core to his mission. Though he was God, he "emptied" himself and became a servant (Philippians 2:5-7). And we're to do the same:

Be imitators of God, as beloved children. And walk in love, as Christ loved us and gave himself up for us, a fragrant offering and sacrifice to God. (Ephesians 5:1-2)

Jesus gave himself in his incarnation, his sinless life, and in his death. And what did his giving accomplish? Salvation for us, glory for God, and great joy for him.

In following Jesus, we must know that it means giving. Giving is how we follow Jesus. This is tough, because living as a giving servant is difficult:

> So therefore, any one of you who does not renounce all that he has cannot be my disciple. (Luke 14:33)

If we're to be like Jesus, we will give.

4. *Walking by Faith Is the Way We Live*

We'll give as we should only if we believe that God will take care of us as he promised:

> And my God will supply every need of yours according to his riches in glory in Christ Jesus. (Philippians 4:19)

Walking by faith means depending on God's care. If we don't live in light of God's promises, we'll hoard for ourselves and not give. If, on the other hand, we're content with God's care and provision, we will give. Giving demonstrates that we trust in God, not in earthly riches:

> The LORD is my shepherd; I shall not want. (Psalm 23:1)

> And God is able to make all grace abound to you, so that having all sufficiency in all things at all times, you may abound in every good work. (2 Corinthians 9:8)

We cannot give the way we should if we're not walking by faith. Giving shows that God is our hope and satisfaction.

What is the result of a gospel-first, missional, I-want-to-be-like-Jesus, walk-by-faith life?

We *give*.

Why do you spend your money for that which is not bread,
and your labor for that which does not satisfy?

– Isaiah 55:2 –

HOW MUCH SHOULD I SAVE FOR RETIREMENT?

Given the warnings, instructions, and examples in the Bible, should I fund a retirement account? And if so, how much should I save? Should I build equity in my home? In this age of massive need, is it okay for the Christian to hang on to wealth?

While answering these types of questions isn't simple, it may not be overly complex either. So let me ask the question about saving for retirement in a different way: How much money should be saved for themselves by those who are gospel-saturated and wholly committed to the glory of God and the work of the kingdom?

Saving money so that our bills can be paid when we're unable to work (notice I didn't use the word *retire*) doesn't seem to be wrong. We should attempt to pay our own way. The problems appear when our vision of retirement demands resources that could and should be used to love God and serve others.

It would be great to have a biblical formula to answer the question about retirement savings, but there isn't one. There are, however, some guidelines:

– Love the Lord your God with all your heart and with all your soul and with your entire mind and with all your strength (Luke 10:27).

– Love your neighbor as yourself (Luke 10:27).

– Whether you eat or drink, or whatever you do, do all to the glory of God (1 Corinthians 10:31).

– Be content with God's provision (Matthew 6:25-26).

– Don't love money (Hebrews 13:5).

– Invest in being rich toward God (Luke 12:15-21).

Clearly, this isn't the approach we hear from Wall Street or most money folks. The message from these sources is all about the need to accumulate as much as possible. They tell us that the risks of living too long, unreliable investment returns, or meeting future medical expenses have only one solution: save more. It may seem like we can never save enough.

But adopting this attitude will leave the work of the kingdom unfunded and might put us in Jesus's story of the rich fool (Luke 12:16-21). Again, in the end, we all live out our priorities.

It's also possible to neglect retirement savings in an ungodly way. We might think that by not saving, we're trusting God for the future, while money that could be saved or given away is spent on selfish choices that don't please God or help our neighbor. It's important to prayerfully think through the issue of retirement in a way that keeps life's purpose at the forefront.

How much should I save for later? This is a question that needs to be handled prayerfully, since there's no single correct answer for everyone. For those with modest incomes, the ability to save may be difficult, and their standard of living may be minimal. For others, income may be more than enough to meet their needs.

Starting with a Jesus-is-everything-to-me perspective, our thinking about saving for retirement should be different. For the Christian, life is not about societal norms or the desire to not work or to have a luxurious retirement. It's about living for Jesus 24/7. And Jesus is all about saving the lost and being the anchor of our lives.

Let's look at three overarching issues as we think about saving for retirement:

Retirement Age

It's easy to think that retirement is about a life of ease or simply not working. But that shouldn't be our focus. Our purpose doesn't change once we reach age sixty or sixty-five or seventy, or when we choose to leave employment. From beginning to end, the Christian life is about becoming more like Jesus and living for him:

> And let us not grow weary of doing good, for in due season we will reap, if we do not give up. (Galatians 6:9)

We should follow the psalmist when he said, "Even to old age and gray hairs, O God, do not forsake me, until I proclaim your might to another generation, your power to all those to come" (Psalm 71:18).

The earlier we retire, the more we'll need to accumulate for retirement income. This also means we won't be able to give away as much since we need savings for our own expenses. For example, if someone started saving for retirement at age forty, planned on retiring at age sixty-five, and wanted to create income until age ninety-five, they would need to save 45 percent more every month than the person planning to retire at age seventy. (This assumes a 3 percent inflation rate and a 5 percent return on savings.)

Standard of Living

The cost of one's personal standard of living is another key factor in saving for retirement. The more you spend in retirement, the more you'll need to accumulate. The less you spend, the less you'll need to accumulate.

Living a simplified lifestyle can help us focus on kingdom work and reduce our need to build a massive retirement account. We must make sure we keep our focus on the main thing:

No soldier gets entangled in civilian pursuits, since his aim is to please the one who enlisted him. (2 Timothy 2:4)

Living for Jesus means our lives are focused on the kingdom in *everything*. Raising children, buying a house or car, and thinking about college, our standard of living, and our retirement should be considered carefully. We don't want to move our focus away from the goal.

Let's look at another reality (the math on this is simple): If there are two couples with the same situation, and one couple wants to retire with 30 percent more income than the other couple, they'll need to save 30 percent more every month to get there.

Living by Faith in God's Promises

Here's more for you to pray and fast about. Living by faith in God's promises is where the rubber hits the road for many people.

The dominant school of thought is that you can never save too much for retirement. With all of the unknowns (medical costs, inflation, investment returns, long-term care possibilities, etc.) there's never enough savings. The risk is too great. Responsible people should save as much as they can.

In response to this let me ask a question and make an observation:

Question: Are missionaries wrong for giving their lives to spreading the gospel and saving little for retirement? If you say no, then another question must be asked: Aren't we all called to live lives of faith and give everything we are to God's mission for us?

While this doesn't mean we shouldn't save for retirement, it does mean that we should always live for the kingdom and not for our wealth.

Observation: For many, giving as much as possible is a lower priority than saving for retirement. Rather than giving as much as we can, it's easy to ask, How much *must* I give? This is simply not the right way to live out our walk with Jesus. As we live in faith, God has promised to be all we need, and walking by faith means that we believe this and act accordingly.

Saving for retirement is important. We should be able to pay our way when we can't work. For the Christian, however, retiring to an early cushy lifestyle should not be our focus. We should continue to live for Jesus and work to advance his kingdom.

Live small, give much, trust God.

Finishing life to the glory of Christ means resolutely resisting the typical American dream of retirement. It means being so satisfied with all that God promises to be for us in Christ that we are set free from the cravings that create so much emptiness and uselessness in retirement. Instead, knowing that we have an infinitely satisfying and everlasting inheritance in God just over the horizon of life makes us zealous in our few remaining years here to spend ourselves in the sacrifices of love, not the accumulation of comforts.

– John Piper –

What About Differing Priorities?

What if my spouse and I have different financial priorities? It's important to be careful with this. Disagreement can lead to incorrect assumptions about the other person's motives and spiritual maturity. Two people can have the same overarching goal – to glorify God in every aspect of life and live as stewards – and still disagree about how to allocate their income.

This disagreement may be a good thing. It can serve to slow us down so we can prayerfully consider decisions before making them. Your spouse's thinking may take into account something that you should rethink. Above all, know that God, in his sovereignty, has put this differing opinion in front of you for a reason. Don't simply discount your spouse. Engage as someone who cares about him or her. Make sure you understand your spouse's perspective before assuming your opinion on the matter is God-honoring and your spouse's is not.

There can, however, be situations where motives are clearly not God-honoring, and the core issue is deeper than one's perspective or personality. These are bigger issues than how to handle money, and it's common to see greed, a worldly focus, pride, and other sins holding sway.

While it's impossible to deal with all of this here, I'll share three critical actions to help a spouse with little inclination toward stewardship:

1. Pray for your spouse and pray for yourself. It always starts and ends with prayer.

2. Live a walk of biblical faith where your spouse can see the results of trusting a faithful God.

3. Consistently attend a biblically faithful church where your spouse can be encouraged by biblical preaching, interaction with other disciples, and witnessing Christians responding to God's leading.

THINKING ABOUT COLLEGE COSTS

Before we discuss funding college costs, I need to say this: due to the game-changing amount of money that hangs in the balance, thinking correctly about college and college costs is critically important. Let me mention five controlling concepts that can easily influence our decisions in this area:

1. *Societal influence.* Today's culture often considers an expensive college diploma to be a sign of prestige or intelligence.

2. *Parental guilt.* Often we adopt the position that, for our children, cost shouldn't be a consideration. We feel guilty thinking about the money when our child's future is at stake. Even if the child doesn't appreciate the need for college or really have the aptitude to do well, there's a belief that he or she will be thankful and find it useful later.

3. *Easy money.* Often, just by doing a little work online, we can access thousands of dollars for college through loans. We might conclude that our child can get the college experience today, with no worries about paying the bill until later.

4. *Earning potential.* We may be convinced that pursuing a college degree will unquestionably increase a child's income in the future.

5. *Intangible benefits.* What's the real value of a college education? The benefits of college life and training your brain to think

at a higher level can add to a person's life in ways that can't be measured.

The impact of college costs can stay with us and our children for decades, so prayer and a focus on one's calling are vital. College debt not only creates day-to-day financial stress but also can inhibit our ability to follow the call of Christ in the future because we've burdened ourselves with debt payments and won't have the financial flexibility to follow God's leading.

Please don't misunderstand; I'm not against college. And for some professions, such as being a medical doctor, lawyer, or CPA, some debt may be appropriate.[20] I am, however, against being blindly controlled by simple perceptions in the decision-making process. There are many, many parents and children who are enslaved to the debt that follows college. And there are many, many parents and children who've paid thousands of dollars in tuition when the money could have been put to better use.

Let me suggest four critical steps as you consider college for yourself, your spouse, or your child:

1. Pray that God would give clarity in thinking about college. We need to see this issue in a way that's Christ-exalting. We need faith to trust God in all things.

2. If you're a parent, prayerfully develop your college convictions long before you actually face the issue. This way you can start guiding your child's thinking early. Don't wait to come up with a game plan until you're in an emotional discussion with your child about the college adventure (I did this, and it was terrible).

3. Get specific about tuition. How much will it cost and where will the money come from? If your answer is loans, make sure you have a plan for debt payment, and prayerfully

consider alternatives. Don't simply jump into debt thinking that it will just work out somehow. When it comes to debt, a we'll-worry-about-it-later attitude often ends in great pain.

4. If you're a parent, be careful when considering cosigning for your child's student loans. This can be difficult, but please understand the possible and often likely outcome here. You may end up paying tens of thousands of dollars that you can't afford.

As a father of four, I've walked through this difficult issue and made mistakes in the process. Communicating your convictions early and often is critical.

IS IT WRONG TO OWN STOCKS?

Let me try to clarify the question of investing in stocks by rephrasing it this way: Is it immoral to buy or own individual stocks or stock funds? Often, this question comes from two perspectives: risk and morality.

(Please know that nothing I write here should be construed as investment advice. That's a different thing entirely. Also, when I mention investing in stocks, unless I state otherwise, assume that I mean stock funds, not individual stocks.)

Risk

The market can and does decline. So is it good stewardship to take the risk that comes with stock ownership?

There's no doubt that many people have lost money in the stock market. But it's not as simple as saying the stock market is a bad place for my money. No matter where a person puts their money, risk is present. When we leave it in the bank, inflation can erode its buying power. So the "safe" places tend to lose value slowly over time. On the other hand, real estate and stocks and bonds can experience significant fluctuations in value. Over time, however, they've outperformed the "safe" stuff.

With stocks (equities) or stock funds, it's critically important to think long-term. If you can't stay invested seven to ten years or more, don't consider stocks.

It's relatively easy to say that someone young might want to invest their long-term money in stocks. Mistakes are often made, however, when one is older. The thought might be that at some age – perhaps sixty-five or seventy – a regular paycheck will stop; therefore, because of the risk, we should have no money in the market. This assumes that all of one's money will be needed in the next ten years. Because that's probably not true, it may be appropriate that some long-term money – even at age sixty-five – be invested in conservative stocks.

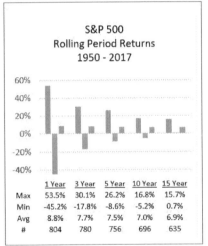

The accompanying chart gives you an idea of how stocks have performed over different time frames.

Morality

The moral objection to owning stocks is much more complicated. The concern is that by owning stock in a particular company or sector, I'm supporting or profiting from the sinful activity of that company or industry. The danger here is that we settle for simple and naive thinking.

The reality is that we cannot be completely removed from mingling our efforts or money with the world around us. God has integrated us into the fabric of this world. If you work for a business you don't own, your efforts contribute to the profits and objectives of your employer. If you buy groceries at a store, you support those who own the store and the employees who work there. When you buy a car, you reward the manufacturer, dealership, and countless others in the product chain. And many of these folks, if not most of them, live godless lives.

I don't wish to make this question more difficult or complex than it needs to be, nor do I want us to throw up our hands and not think about how we invest. Rather, I mention these things because the better informed we are, the better we can pray and act.

When it comes to owning stock, there's a continuum of participation in the profits:

1. You may be a majority owner of a business or on the board of directors. This is a position of direct control. You're directly connected to the vision and success of the business and will profit from its activity. In this position, you have a decision-making role in the product, the manufacturing, the marketing, and the sales. You not only profit, but you create the profit.

2. You may own a significant but minor interest in a business. Often this still gives you a platform for real input that can have an impact on the activities of the business. You're an influential owner.

3. You may be the passive owner of a small amount of company stock. While you may not be interested in

influencing company operations, you're hoping to profit from what the business does. You have the choice to align with the business by owning its stock or not.

4. You could own shares of a fund that owns the stock of many different companies. Some of these fund managers take an active role in the companies the fund owns. These funds usually have published guidelines helping you understand how the fund operates and what type of companies it will own.

5. You could own shares of a fund where management is passive, like an index fund. Here the fund management is simply looking to participate in the returns that a group of similar stocks will create. The manager often has a broad range of stock categories to choose from, such as large U.S. companies, foreign stocks, technology stocks, high dividend paying companies, and so on.

6. There are funds where management screens the companies that the fund will own in order to eliminate those businesses that move against a certain set of values.

I certainly believe that it's wrong to own the individual stock of a company that overtly moves against biblical values. Here we're directly profiting from godless activity while having complete control over whether we own the stock.

While owning equities can be appropriate and helpful under the right conditions, we need to prayerfully think through the moral issues here. Choosing to not think about things isn't the same as acting in ignorance. We are responsible.

The call to holiness while living in a fallen world can be a challenge. It's not always simple. But we do have Jesus as our example, all of Scripture for wisdom, and the Holy Spirit as our guide.

Is It a Sin to Be Rich?

Because we know that God's gifts are to be used to bring him glory and further the kingdom, the question of whether it's wrong to be rich seems natural. But the answer isn't quite as simple as a yes or a no.

While the simplest answer must be no, it's not a sin to be rich. It's vital that we examine all of Scripture here. In 1 Timothy, Paul tells us that the rich are not to trust in their riches:

> As for the rich in this present age, charge them not to be haughty, nor to set their hopes on the uncertainty of riches, but on God, who richly provides us with everything to enjoy. (1 Timothy 6:17)

So being the object of God's financial generosity is not sin, but responding wrongly is. It's easy, however, to pull this verse from Scripture and reach a wrong conclusion, such as: since being rich isn't wrong, it stands to reason that it's okay to strive to be rich. Such is the power of money; it pulls at us and bends us toward sin rather than faithfulness.

We should read and understand 1 Timothy 6:17 along with passages that warn us about the dangers of money and the ruin it can bring (Matthew 6:19-21; Hebrews 13:5; Proverbs 23:4). After all, a little before 1 Timothy 6:17 we read these verses:

> Those who desire to be rich fall into temptation, into a snare, into many senseless and harmful desires that plunge people into ruin and destruction. For the love of money is a root of all kinds of evils. It is through this craving that some have wandered away from the faith and pierced themselves with many pangs. (1 Timothy 6:9-10)

And don't forget about Luke 12:13-21, the parable of the rich fool.

So how does all this work? How can one *be* rich without *striving* to get rich? How can I have more than I need while knowing that my wealth could feed the hungry, clothe the naked, care for families in need, or fund evangelistic efforts?

Two examples might help here:

First, a business owner might own a business that generates income for his or her family. The business not only generates income, but the business itself has value. It might be worth a few million dollars, so the owner is rich, and the business produces income for the owner and hopefully for many others. The business owner is rich, but the asset (like a farmer's land) is needed to generate the income. Is it wrong for this business owner to develop the business? No, the business should be developed. However, this business and its income should be used to serve the kingdom.

Another example is the retirement plan that many of us maintain. This is a reserve designed to help us pay the bills when we cannot work. Because of this money, we have more than is needed to meet today's needs. We're rich. Is it wrong to have a retirement plan? No. We must, however, be prayerful as we think about this. Thoughts of retirement and a faithless future lifestyle can easily harden us against the leading of the Holy Spirit.

Remember, while it isn't a sin to have more than we need, it all belongs to God. We're called to live by faith in this world that is not our home.

Another important question might be: Is it okay to live an inflated, lavish lifestyle that spends resources without regard to Christian stewardship? The answer here is clearly no.

Is This Purchase Appropriate?

At times, the discussion of stewardship and priorities still isn't enough. Assuming we want to live Christ-exalting lives, how might we think through a possible purchase?

These four questions can help in the decision-making:

1. Does this purchase directly support my life's purpose? If I want my life to be all about loving God and my neighbor, will this help?

   You shall love the Lord your God with all your heart and with all your soul and with all your strength and with all your mind, and your neighbor as yourself. (Luke 10:27)

2. Does this purchase bolster my ego or pride?

   Do nothing from selfish ambition or conceit, but in humility count others more significant than yourselves. Let each of you look not only to his own interests, but also to the interests of others. (Philippians 2:3-4)

3. Will this purchase cause others to question my values and priorities? As we live our lives and make spending decisions, we communicate our values and beliefs. Does this purchase send the right message?

   So, whether you eat or drink, or whatever you do, do all to the glory of God. (1 Corinthians 10:31)

4. Would this purchase align with the choices other faith-filled believers might make? Would I recommend that others follow my example?

   Remember your leaders, those who spoke to you the word of God. Consider the outcome of their way of life, and imitate their faith. (Hebrews 13:7)

Should I Pay Off Debt, or Build a Reserve?

Because those with too much consumer debt (credit cards, student loans, auto loans) often don't have a reserve, this question comes to the forefront: Should we first pay off debt, or try to build a reserve at the same time?

In facing this difficult situation, I've found that the best strategy is to first commit to no unnecessary spending. Second, focus on paying down the credit card. Third, if an unforeseen necessary expense occurs, use the credit card. Fourth, build a reserve after the debt is paid off.

Making a suggestion to use the credit card may sound strange when you're trying to get rid of debt, but follow the logic, and I think it will make sense. In a situation with credit card debt and no reserve, giving priority to creating a reserve can keep the credit card active and generating interest charges longer than it should.

Let's say you have $10,000 in credit card debt and no reserve. If, through spending adjustments, you have an extra $500 at the end of the first month, I would apply that to the credit card debt rather than to a reserve.

Let's assume that this happens for the next three months also. You still don't have a reserve, but the credit card balance is now down to $8,000.[21]

Then you incur a $750 car repair bill, which you pay for with the credit card. With that repair charge, the credit card balance now rises to $8,750. But this is better than having a $2,000 reserve ($500 monthly for four months) and $10,000 of credit card debt plus the related interest charges.

APPLICATION

What questions or issues mentioned in this chapter do you struggle with?

5

Take Action

Ten Steps to Move Us Forward

Step five in winning the money battle is taking action. Because we live out what we believe, the critical work of financial planning is done in the heart. But living it out means *action*:

> Be doers of the word, and not hearers only, deceiving yourselves. (James 1:22)

So this chapter has ten actions that can help move us in the right direction.

TEN STEPS

1. Pray

Praying can, at least to some extent, be reduced to two important things: what we care about, and who we're trusting for what we care about.

If for example, we care deeply about how we handle our money and we think the answer is only about self-discipline, we probably won't pray much. But if we care deeply about how we handle our money and also know that only God can work this out for his glory, we'll pray all the time.

As you know, living a life of love and faithfulness for Jesus is a battle. Evil will attempt to pull us away. So as you study the Bible, pray...

— that God would enlarge the beauty of the gospel in your life.

— that God would convict of sin and grant repentance.

— that God would provide clarity for needed action and the faith to trust him as you follow.

2. Create a Functional Budget

A budget is more than knowing where you're spending money. A budget should require you to think as you spend. It should have a real-time connection to your money. Because many budgets don't have this connection, they often don't help the way they should.

When I was younger (pre-computer), the "envelope" budget was common. As each paycheck was cashed, the appropriated amount of money was deposited into separate envelopes labeled "transportation," "entertainment/eating out," "food," "rent," "Christmas," "emergencies," and other things. As various expenses needed to be paid, the money was removed from the appropriate envelope. It was a functional budget.

At the beginning of the month, the envelopes were full of money, and I knew the bills could be paid. There were times, however, when certain envelopes – such as the one for entertainment and eating out – were empty before the end of the month. If we wanted to go out to eat and we didn't have enough money in the envelope, it was decision time. What do we do? Do we have a "slush" envelope to take money from? Do we borrow from another envelope? Do we use a credit card? Do we stay home? Through the use of a functional budget, we were forced to confront our spending habits and make informed decisions.

There are some who love the details of a complex budget, but I don't. It can feel overwhelming, time-sucking, and absolutely not fun. It's often unworkable. So while there may be many budgeting tools available, I'd like to share a simple, functional budgeting approach that almost anyone can implement.

In its simplest form, this functional budget requires a few different checking accounts at the same bank, in case you need to transfer money from one account to the other. We're using checking accounts here instead of envelopes.

Here's an example of how this might work. Ben and Jill have separated their budget into eight different categories:

1. Predictable monthly expenses (mortgage, utilities, giving, telephone, etc.).

2. Transportation (fuel, car maintenance, insurance, car payment, etc.).

3. Necessary but variable needs (groceries, clothing, dog food, toiletries, etc.).

4. Medical costs (deductibles, copays, etc.).

5. Emergency reserve.

6. Gifts (Christmas, birthdays, anniversaries, etc.).

7. Vacations.

8. Discretionary spending (eating out, entertainment, etc.).

They've also opened eight different checking accounts at their local bank corresponding to those categories.

Every time they get paid, they allocate enough money to each account in order to pay the expenses connected to that account. If done correctly, this means all the bills get paid without worry.

Let's look at two of their accounts:

In the "Predictable Monthly Expenses" account, those expenses might look like this:

> Mortgage: $1,250
>
> Life insurance: $50
>
> Church: $1,000
>
> Telephone: $75
>
> Utilities: water, $25; electricity, $50; natural gas, $70
>
> Cable: $125
>
> *Total*: $2,645

This "Predictable Monthly Expenses" checking account will have $2,645 going into it each month, and $2,645 leaving it each month.

Since payments from this account will vary in amount and payment date, it can be important to have some excess or "float" in the account so everything gets paid without running out of money.

Now let's look at the "Transportation" account:

> Car payment: $300
>
> Maintenance and repairs: $150
>
> Fuel: $150
>
> Licenses: $25
>
> Insurance: $150
>
> Next car: $100
>
> *Total*: $875

For an item like car maintenance and repairs, the expenses don't normally follow a predictable schedule, but a reasonable amount is regularly designated for it. Likewise, fuel costs can widely vary according to how much we drive. These factors mean that Ben and Jill will want to carry a surplus in this account.

Because this is a functional budget, if Ben and Jill want to upgrade their furniture, they'll need to find the money for it. In their current budget, all the money is allocated. So where will the money come from? Is there a "slush" account, and is there enough money in it? If not, they'll need to talk about their need for furniture and make a conscious, informed decision. Maybe, instead of buying now, they accumulate the needed money in one of the checking accounts. Or maybe they have a separate checking account where they build funds for future purchases.

(For a more detailed explanation of how you can put together an easy, functional budget, I encourage you to watch the budgeting video at moneyandthegospel.com.)

3. Adjust Decisively

If your financial situation needs adjusting, adjust it. This may take courage, but we need to be good stewards of God's resources. If spending needs to be reduced, reduce it. If "toys" need to be sold, sell them. Financial problems don't just fix themselves, and following Jesus is not a matter of small adjustments.

Too often people borrow to meet expenses because they hope things will turn around. This is not a good strategy. Debt can build quickly and take years to pay off.

Some adjustments can be almost painless, like shopping for lower insurance rates or cutting back on eating out or looking for sales. Often, however, we just can't face the reality that major adjustments like downsizing the house or taking on a second job are needed.

4. Write It Down

As you write down your priorities, you're actually creating a tool through which you can measure your financial progress and hold yourself accountable. If you're married, it's important that your spouse be included in this process. Things are much easier if you're both on the same page with the plan. While we want to keep this simple, the point here is to create a strategy for moving forward successfully.

Here's an example of how you might do this:

Step 1. Write down your current income and expenses. (Feel free to use the Income and Expense Report you can find at moneyandthegospel.com.)

Step 2. List your financial priorities. They might include things like:

- Buy a house: $25,000 down payment needed.
- Save for the next car: $10,000.
- Give more to the church: $250 monthly.
- Pay off debt: $25,000 ($7,000 credit cards, $6,000 car loan, $12,000 student loan).
- Save for college.
- Reduce spending.
- Save for retirement.
- Create a reserve.

Step 3. Prioritize your priorities according to urgency. It might look like this:

Near-term:

- Reduce spending.
- Pay off debt.
- Give more to the church.

Next-step goals:

– Create a reserve.

– Save for a house purchase.

– Save for the next car.

Long-term goals:

– Save for college.

– Save for retirement.

Step 4. Create a twelve-month action plan for your near-term goals:

Reduce spending:

– Eat out no more than once a week and plan for low-cost, eat-at-home alternatives.

– Allocate a fixed amount of money per paycheck for personal spending.

– Buy only what's needed, and buy things on sale whenever possible.

– Evaluate current insurance costs (auto, homeowners, life, etc.).

– Look at refinancing the mortgage at a lower interest rate.

– NEVER use the credit card.

Pay off debt:

– Implement "snowball" debt reduction with half of any surplus cash flow.

Give more to the church:

– Increase giving to the church with half of any surplus cash flow from the reduction of spending.

Step 5. After a year of success on the twelve-month plan, go back to step #1 and do it all over again.

5. Become Accountable

Being accountable isn't easy. In many ways, this is where the rubber hits the road. Sharing your convictions and commitments with someone else may be just what's needed to help you follow through.

6. Rethink Debt

Are you spending more than you're making? If the answer's yes, the bright red emergency light is flashing. If this financial situation was a medical condition, surgery would be needed—not a Band-Aid. In this situation, you're either spending your savings or taking on debt.

When people buy things based on an affordable credit card payment, they're often on the road to destruction. While the problem may be circumstantial (the car breaks down and needs major repairs) or ignorance (lack of prudent planning skills), it's often spiritual. Greed and idolatry can easily be at the root of the problem.

Often, the reason we buy with borrowed money is that we don't have cash. The reason we don't have the cash may be that we spend too much on things we don't need. And the downward spiral begins. We didn't have the money to pay for what we bought, and now we have additional debt-service payments to make. And now, what if there's another emergency? Where will the money for it come from? More debt?

Using debt can be the road to financial tragedy. The problem can develop quickly and take years to clean up. And debt problems usually bring other troubles as well, like marital stress, poor performance at work, and debt collectors. It's also common for our spiritual growth to stagnate because we aren't being faithful stewards. And the sad truth is that many refuse to do anything about their debt. They can't bring themselves to do surgery on their finances.

Some may have their debt "under control." The debt payments are in their budget, and it seems to be working. Please consider getting rid of your debt anyway (the mortgage may be an exception). Here are three reasons why you should get rid of debt:

1. Debt can be a symptom of sin. While not all debt is sinful, if we make purchases that aren't necessary when we don't have the money to buy the items outright, we should question our hearts. Are we covetous? Do we trust God the way we should? Are we content with God's provision?

2. Debt can encourage us to think in a self-centered, faithless way rather than biblically. Just because we can afford the debt doesn't mean all is good and we should buy. All of our money is God's money.

3. Interest charges increase the cost of the things we buy, and debt can enslave. Even though the debt might be manageable now, it's still one more budget item that must be paid. There's less flexibility to reduce income or allocate money to other priorities. Debt is baggage that can hinder our ability to follow God's call.

In Randy Alcorn's *Managing God's Money,* he challenges his readers to think about the statements we may be making when we go into debt:[22]

– We need more than God has given us.

– God doesn't know best what our needs are.

– God has failed to provide for our needs, forcing us to take matters into our own hands.

– If God doesn't come through the way we think he should, we can find another way.

– Just because today's income is sufficient to make our debt payments, tomorrow's will be too.

7. Update Your Insurances

Insurance is not an exciting subject (at least I don't think so), but it's important. I have a love-hate relationship with insurance as I pay money to have it while hoping I won't use it.

While I won't address all the different types of insurance here, I would like to address a question that confuses many. how much life insurance should we have? A few years ago, I looked through my client files to see if I could come up with a simple rule of thumb that was fairly reliable as an answer to this question. Here's what I found.

For income replacement only (life insurance can be used to meet other needs), the amount should be eight to ten times one's annual income, plus the cost of extra obligations you'd like to fund if you should die (things like college, weddings, consumer debt, mortgage, etc.). From this total, subtract whatever long-term savings we have.

Let's say:

- I make $60,000 per year;
- I have two children, and for their college, I'd like to pay $10,000 annually for four years for each child;
- I have a mortgage of $150,000 that I'd like my wife to be able to pay off if I die;
- and we've saved $50,000 in our retirement plans.

The calculation would be as follows.

$60,000 x 8 =	$480,000
college:	$80,000
mortgage:	$150,000
subtotal:	$710,000
less savings	− $50,000
Current life insurance need:	**$660,000**

By these calculations, I need about $660,000 of life insurance today. That may seem like a large amount, but remember:

- My obligations are pretty big, and we haven't saved a great deal.
- As time passes and, God willing, the obligations decline (mortgage principal decreases, and children finish college) and our savings increase, the amount of life insurance I need for income replacement should go down and eventually disappear.

I have also illustrated my future need if, in fifteen years, my financial situation has developed based on the assumptions mentioned above:

$$\$80,000 \times 8 = \$640,000$$

college:	0
mortgage:	$\underline{\$100,000}$
subtotal:	$\$740,000$
less savings	$\underline{-\$250,000}$
Life insurance need in 15 years:	**$490,000**

You can see, as my obligations decline and my savings increase, my life insurance need could decline.

This formula isn't perfect, but I've found it to be a good starting point.

Just a note: If your lifestyle is extremely frugal, the initial multiplier could be reduced from eight to six times your earnings. Also, if you're young, just married, and without children, your life insurance needs may be minimal since the ongoing obligations, should you die, are minimal.

8. Simplify Your Lifestyle

With cars, internet, vacations, computers, cell phones, medical costs, entertainment, eating out, toys, clothes, pets, houses, real estate taxes, insurance, upkeep on the stuff we own, and so on, we spend lots of money. We each have a certain personal standard of living or, as I call it, a lifestyle disposition.

I use that term *lifestyle disposition* because it goes beyond money. It includes the far-reaching effects of our spending habits on our time, energy, health, availability, and so forth – all of which are valuable resources that can either serve our priorities or not.

The Bible seems to address "simplicity" through the example of Jesus and the need for believers to have a singular focus in life. It's important to have a life that isn't compromised by distracting thoughts, sin, wrong motives, or too much stuff. Instead, we should have a life all about living for Jesus.[23]

In his book *Margin*, Richard Swenson makes this interesting observation about Jesus:

> *He was born with nothing, lived with little, and died with nothing. His simplicity was not accidental. Jesus could have chosen any standard, yet he chose to live simply.*[24]

There's only so much "space" in our lives. Through a simplified lifestyle, we can use more of that space for the mission we're on. If we long to be engaged in serving Jesus with all we have and are, we need to get rid of things that would slow us down:

If we have food and clothing, with these we will be content. (1 Timothy 6:8)

Let us also lay aside every weight, and sin which clings so closely, and let us run with endurance the race that is set before us. (Hebrews 12:1)

No soldier gets entangled in civilian pursuits, since his aim is to please the one who enlisted him. (2 Timothy 2:4)

9. Build a Reserve

Everyone needs a cash reserve. If the unexpected happens and my budget can't handle it, a reserve is needed. Using credit cards as that reserve will only put you on the road to disaster.

10. Know Your Numbers

Most of us think we should put something away for later. And with people living longer, the amount it takes to pay your own way can be big.

Let's say, all things considered, I'm shooting for a retirement plan balance of $500,000, and I have thirty years to get there. I assume an investment return of 5 percent per year. That means I would need to save about $598 each month.

Is that a "good" monthly savings goal? Well, let's make an adjustment in the assumptions. It might be fair to assume that I'll be able to save more in the future because my income may increase. If I assume that my income will go up 2 percent a year, and that therefore I can save 2 percent more each year, how does that change things? The amount I now need to save today is about $476 monthly – $122 less per month. So that's better. But it's still quite a bit of money.

Let's add another adjustment to the scenario. What if I worked two extra years? This means I have two additional years to fund and grow the retirement account and two fewer years to draw income from the account. How much difference would that make? Now we need to save about $439 monthly—$159 less per month than the original $598.[25]

Let's make one more adjustment. Suppose I went through the budget and found ways to spend less. Through this process, I discovered I could also reduce the annual income we'll need for retirement by 10 percent. How does this affect the amount we'll need to save? Now it's about $395 each month—$203 per month less than the original $598.

Depending on the assumptions we're willing to make, we may be able to reduce it even further. For example, if we assume that we can save 20 percent more in the fifteen years just before retirement (mostly because family expenses will decline, and we may be in our peak earning years), the amount we need to save today goes down to $372 monthly, which is $226 per month less than that original $598.

One objection to this way of thinking revolves around the many financial risks on the way to retirement – such as living longer than expected, increasing medical costs, inflation, increased long-term care costs, or sub-par investment returns. So the inclination is to save as much as possible – period. The prevailing thought is that you just can't have too much in your retirement account.

Be careful here. We don't want to have the mindset of the rich man in Luke 12:15-21. We don't want to focus on retirement and live as if our faith is in our money. We also have other important priorities, right? Like funding our churches and sending the gospel to those who haven't heard.

I also find it interesting that while many object to saving less for retirement so they can give more to the kingdom, they don't hesitate to buy expensive cars and take expensive vacations.

It's all about the priorities.

APPLICATION

What three financial changes do you need to make now?

1.

2.

3.

Appendix

FINANCIAL PRIORITIES REPORT

Following are several financial priorities, plus space for you to add one of your own. How do these priorities figure personally in your life?

In the space beside each item, rank each of them in priority order from 1 (most important) to 15 (least important).

____ Buy a car

____ Pay for college

____ Save more for retirement

____ Buy life insurance

____ Give more to church and charity

____ Change housing

____ Reduce debt

____ Find a new or additional job

____ Get a will, healthcare power of attorney, etc.

____ Develop an investment strategy

____ Reduce spending

____ Review insurances

____ Create a budget

____ Provide financial help for children or parents

____ *other:*

FINANCIAL ASSESSMENT REPORT

For each of the statements below, record the number that best reflects your response:

1 = *disagree*
2 = *somewhat disagree*
3 = *somewhat agree*
4 = *strongly agree*

_____ My spouse and I have the same financial priorities.

_____ My/our financial priorities need adjustment.

_____ I/we have a budget.

_____ I/we have too much debt.

_____ I/we spend too much money on unnecessary things.

_____ I/we have concerns about college costs.

_____ I/we have concerns about retirement.

_____ I/we have questions or concerns about life insurance or estate planning.

_____ My/our need is more current income.

What is your main financial concern at this time? Write your answer in the space below:

About the Author

Waldean Wall works in the financial planning industry. With a background in income tax and small business development, he was a personal adviser for twenty years and is now a national speaker to brokers, CPAs, insurance specialists, and financial planners. He teaches tax, retirement, and estate planning strategies.

- ChFC (Chartered Financial Consultant), American College, Bryn Mawr, PA
- MATS, Bethel Seminary, St. Paul, MN
- MSFS, Institute of Business & Finance, San Diego, CA
- EA (Enrolled Agent), Admitted to practice before the IRS

Moneyandthegospel.com is the website where you can go for email updates and social media access.

Notes

[1] John 17:3.

[2] Also see: John 3:16; Romans 4:25; 1 Timothy 1:15; Hebrews 9:28; 1 Peter 2:24; 3:18; 1 John 4:10.

[3] Also: Genesis 14:19; Exodus 19:5; Leviticus 25:23; Deuteronomy 10:14; 1 Chronicles 29:11; Psalms 24:1; 50:10; 95:4-5; 89:11; Isaiah 43:6-7; Haggai 2:8; Romans 11:36; 1 Corinthians 6:19-20; Colossians 1:16-17.

[4] Also: Genesis 26:12-13; Deuteronomy 8:18; 1 Chronicles 29:12-14; Job 1:21; Psalm 23:1; Daniel 4:25; Hosea 2:8; Matthew 6:33; Mark 10:29-30; Luke 6:38; John 3:27; 6:65; Romans 12:3; 12:6; 1 Corinthians 4:7; 2 Corinthians 9:8; Ephesians 3:16; Philippians 4:19; James 1:17; 1 Peter 4:10; 2 Peter 1:3.

[5] Also: Genesis 2:15; Matthew 5:16; 24:45-51; Luke 16:11; Romans 12:1; 1 Corinthians 4:1-2; 6:20; 10:31; 2 Corinthians 9:11; Ephesians 2:10; Philippians 1:11; Colossians 3:23; 1 Peter 4:10-11; Titus 1:7; 1 Peter 4:11.

[6] Also: Psalm 66:18; Proverbs 28:9; John 9:33; 1John 3:21.

[7] John Piper, *Desiring God* (Sisters, Oregon: Multnomah, 2003), 197.

[8] Matthew 11:25; 1 Corinthians 1:19-31; Job 37:24.

[9] Philippians 2:6-7.

[10] Giving is not limited to money from those who are wealthy. Everyone gives. We give of what God has given us (1 Peter 4:10-12).

[11] David Mathis, *Habits of Grace: Enjoying Jesus through the Spiritual Disciplines* (Wheaton, Illinois: Crossway, 2016), 209.

[12] Also: Proverbs 3:7; Isaiah 5:21; Romans 1:22; 12:16; 1 Corinthians 1:20; 1:27.

[13] Also: Matthew 6:25; 10:28; 20:26-28; 23:12; Mark 8:34-38; Luke 9:23.

[14] Matthew 11:30.

[15] Also: Proverbs 4:23; 21:2; 21:23; 21:26; Psalm 51:10; Romans 12:2.

[16] Jon Bloom, *Things Not Seen: A Fresh Look at Old Stories of Trusting God's Promises* (Wheaton, Illinois: Crossway, 2015), 171.

[17] Ivan Mesa, "How to Honor Your Maker with Your Wallet," https://www.thegospelcoalition.org/article/how-you-honor-your-maker-with-your-wallet/.

[18] Romans 6:6-14; Philippians 1:6.

[19] David Mathis, "Greed," in *Killjoys: The Seven Deadly Sins*, edited by Marshall Segal (Minneapolis: Desiring God, 2015), 71-72.

[20] Even in these professions there are often ways to gain access to a great education without going into debt.

[21] This would actually be more than $8,000 due to accumulating interest charges.

[22] Randy Alcorn, *Managing God's Money: A Biblical Guide* (Carol Stream, Illinois: Tyndale, 2011), 170.

[23] Also: Psalm 1:2; Joshua 1:8; Matthew 6:24; 1 Corinthians 7:35; 2 Timothy 2:4.

[24] Richard A. Swenson, *Margin: Restoring Emotional, Physical, Financial, and Time Reserves to Overloaded Lives* (Colorado Springs: NavPress, 2004), 171.

[25] In an actual analysis, the number could be even lower due to the way Social Security retirement income works. If we delay taking the benefit for two years, it will be more when we start receiving it. If we don't delay Social Security and take it before we need it, we may have another source of income we can save for retirement.

39911850R00080

Made in the USA
Middletown, DE
21 March 2019